The First Ships Around the World

W. D. Brownlee

MASTER MARINER

Published in cooperation with Cambridge University Press
Lerner Publications Company, Minneapolis

Editors' Note: In preparing this edition of *The Cambridge Topic Books* for publication, the editors have made only a few minor changes in the original material. In some isolated cases, British spelling and usage were altered in order to avoid possible confusion for our readers. Whenever necessary, information was added to clarify references to people, places, and events in British history. An index was also provided in each volume.

LIBRARY OF CONGRESS CATALOGING IN PUBLICATION DATA

Brownlee, Walter D.
  The first ships around the world.

  (A Cambridge Topic Book)
  Original ed. published under title: The first ships round the world.
  Includes index.
  SUMMARY: Describes the ships of the fourteenth-century and recounts the voyage of Magellan, explaining life aboard the ships and the instruments of navigation.

  1. Magalhâes, Fernão, d. 1521—Juvenile literature. 2. Voyages around the world—Juvenile literature. [1. Ships. 2. Magellan, Ferdinand, d. 1521. 3. Voyages around the world] I. Title.

G420.M2B74 1977   910'.41   76-22430
ISBN 0-8225-1204-1

This edition first published 1977 by Lerner Publications Company by permission of Cambridge University Press.

Original edition copyright © 1974 by Cambridge University Press as part of *The Cambridge Introduction to the History of Mankind: Topic Book* under the title *The First Ships round the World.*

International Standard Book Number: 0-8225-1204-1
Library of Congress Catalog Card Number: 76-22430

Manufactured in the United States of America.

This edition is available exclusively from:
Lerner Publications Company, 241 First Avenue North, Minneapolis, Minnesota 55401

Contents

Introduction

During the fifteenth and sixteenth centuries, sailors from western Europe explored the seas and coasts of almost all the world. They dared to steer outwards, across vast expanses of ocean, and they found many lands and seas whose existence they had not even imagined. This book attempts to explain what it must have been like aboard the ships of those daring sailors: how the ships themselves were designed, how they were navigated, the daily routine, the conditions of life — and death — of the men whose skill and toughness made the great discoveries possible.

THE SHIPS

Fourteenth-century ships

There were two main types of seagoing vessels available when Europeans first began to venture along strange coasts and into unknown waters. The ships were the cog and the early carrack. Neither was suitable for the conditions encountered by the explorers.

The cog – Northern Europe: Baltic Sea and North Sea

The cog was a direct descendant of the Viking trading ship. The hull was clinker-built, with its planks overlapping. This method of building made the hull strong without the need for very large supporting ribs and beams. The cog was a sturdy vessel and could carry a great deal of cargo, but her bulk and draft (depth under water) made her difficult to handle, and with only one square sail she could make little headway against unfavourable winds.

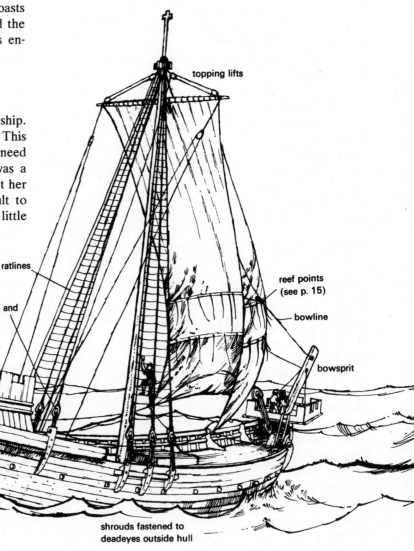

Cog. Northern Europe
mid fourteenth century

topping lifts

ratlines

deadeyes and lanyards

reef points
(see p. 15)

bowline

bowsprit

stern rudder

clinker-built hull

shrouds fastened to deadeyes outside hull

The early carrack—Southern Europe: Mediterranean Sea

Like the cog, the carrack was deep drafted and difficult to handle, especially with a small crew. The small lateen (triangular) sail on the mizzen mast was copied from Arabian ships; it helped to balance the ship and keep her steady on course. The planks of the hull were nailed to the frames and laid side by side to present a smooth surface (carvel-built). The deck beams were large for extra strength and they protruded through the hull, thus helping to hold the vessel together.

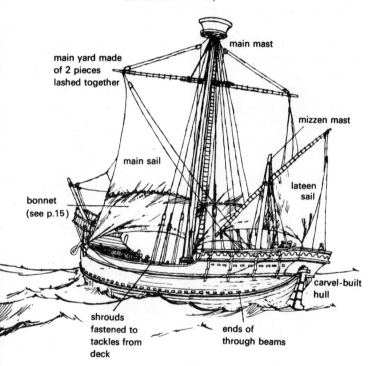

Carrack. Mediterranean
late fourteenth century

main mast

main yard made of 2 pieces lashed together

mizzen mast

main sail

lateen sail

bonnet (see p.15)

carvel-built hull

shrouds fastened to tackles from deck

ends of through beams

Ancestors of cog and carrack. Ships of the North Sea (*above*) and Mediterranean in the thirteenth century.

For exploration a ship was needed that was:
1. Sturdy enough to face the winds, swells, and waves of the deep oceans.
2. Small enough to explore coastal waters and rivers.
3. Large enough to carry supplies and trade goods for a long voyage.
4. Handy enough to be controlled by a small, and possibly weak, crew.

No single ship would ever be capable of fulfilling all the conditions perfectly but both the cog and early carrack had something to give.

Ships fit for the ocean

The first European ocean-crossing vessels

Most ships of this period were built by traditional methods handed from father to son, and often no construction plans existed. A new type of vessel would take many years to evolve – unless someone of great wealth and power was looking for a new ship for a new job. Such a man appeared at the beginning of the fifteenth century. He was Prince Henry of Portugal, known as the Navigator. He was determined to explore the coastline of Africa and then to find a sea route to the riches of the East.

The first of his explorations were carried out by square-sailed ships rather like small cogs, but he developed a more suitable type. This new type, called a caravel, was probably based on the boats used by the Portuguese fishermen.

The caravel

Caravels were the vessels Henry sent out from his port of Sagres, usually working in pairs, to search southwards along the coast of Africa. They were small ships, not too heavy to be rowed when required. On deck would be stored at least four very long oars, or sweeps. Each sweep would be manned by up to four men who would have to walk backwards and forwards to row the ship. The hull was carvel-built but the deck beams did not protrude outside the hull. Caravels rarely had high decks fore and aft, since any high structure would interfere with the sails. As is necessary with lateen rigs, the shrouds led down to the main deck and were tightened by tackles (see p. 12).

The picture shows three lateen sails, but caravels with only two lateen sails were also very common.

The caravel had many good points. The hull design retained the qualities of a good fishing vessel; it was meant for all weathers: it was of shallow draft, strong yet light, easily handled, and fast — even with the wind on the bows. The caravel was an ideal ship for coastal exploration.

Caravel

Approximate dimensions:
Overall length   19 yds (17m)
Greatest breadth   6 yds (5m)
Keel length   12 yds (11m)
Deepest draft   5 ft (1.5m)
Crew of between 20 and 25 men
(Note the low bow and stern.)

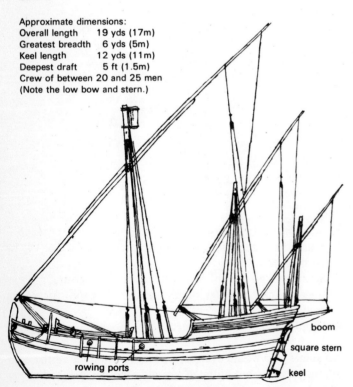

boom

square stern

rowing ports

keel

Manning the sweeps

The sweepmen rowed by walking backwards and forwards, probably keeping time by singing a rhythmic shanty.

The round caravel (caravela redonda)

When a lateen-rigged ship changes tack, or direction, there is hard work for the crew. Not only must the sail and spar be hauled around the mast but the shrouds have to be reset. A square-rigged ship (one with sails set *across* the ship, like the cog) cannot sail as close into the wind as a lateener, but changing tack is simply a matter of swinging the sail around by tackles. Many captains adapted the caravel so that she combined both square and lateen rig. Such a ship was called a caravela redonda. Because the fore mast had been moved right forward, a bowsprit was now used to take a forestay (see p. 9), which helped to hold the mast firm. The bowsprit also took the bowlines, which hauled the sail edge into a position to catch the wind.

Columbus' *Niña* and *Pinta* were originally both lateen-rigged caravels but early in the 1492 voyage they were altered to caravelas redondas.

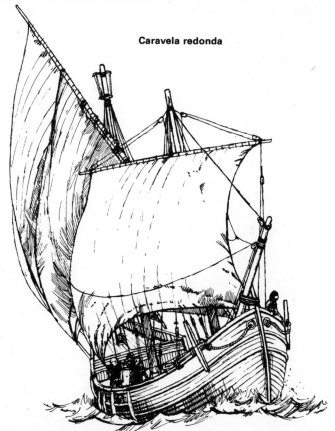

Caravela redonda

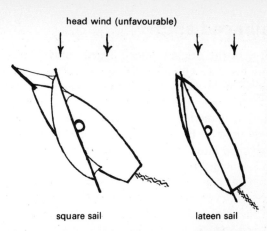

head wind (unfavourable)

square sail   lateen sail

Square Sail. Cannot sail close to wind, probably no closer than 50° in a well balanced ship with an experienced crew. The ship will also make leeway (drift bodily with the wind).

Lateen Sail. Can sail very close to wind indeed and not make much leeway.

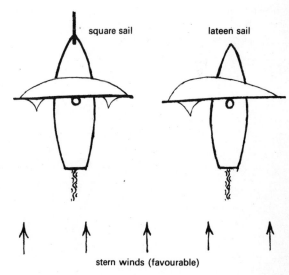

square sail   lateen sail

stern winds (favourable)

Square Sail. Takes full advantage of wind with evenly balanced pressure.

Lateen Sail. Uneven pressure makes ship more difficult to steer.

A balanced ship

The value of the original lateen-rigged caravel for coastal exploration was accepted by all, but for east-west ocean voyages the rig of the caravela redonda was more suited to the steady trade winds. Once the methods of balancing square sails with lateen on three or even four masts were discovered, they were used on bigger ships, too, and the early carrack was developed into a deep-sea, all-weather vessel, which became the standard type for over a century. Indeed, all later developments may be said to be based on this idea. During the sixteenth century the name 'carrack' became reserved for very big ships and did not refer to the rig, since this mixed rig had become so common with ships of all sizes and hull-shapes. Although never as fast as the caravel when the wind was on the beam or forward of the beam, the new carrack type had advantages that were more important.

It was considerably broader yet only a little extra in draft. This meant that far more cargo and stores could be loaded. The ship was stronger and sturdier and could carry cannon with less risk of being strained.

Compared to the slim and swift caravel, the carrack type was somewhat of a fat barrel, but it is possible that the sailors

Balancing with three masts

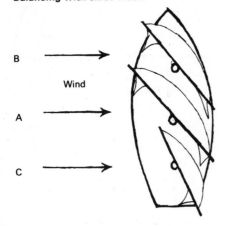

The main power comes from A. In the bows the wind on the fore sail B adds more power but tends to push the ship's head away to leeward. At C the easily adjusted lateen sail balances the force at B.

felt a little more secure in it. Being higher in the stern it ran less risk of being overwhelmed by high waves coming from behind when the wind was very strong. The high forecastle (see p. 9) cut down a little the amount of water thrown over the bows as the ship butted into the waves, and probably made the sailor's life drier and more comfortable. The bowsprit was used to carry a light sail called a spritsail; this was found to add more pulling power and could still be balanced by the lateen aft. Royal ships, and others used in war, had often carried a large flag at the top of the main mast, and this probably resulted in sailors realising that an extra sail could be carried there. So the topsail came into being. It was very small and weak at first and only used in light winds.

It was possible for yet more sail power to be obtained in light following winds. Columbus reports that on one occasion he set all the sails, then set up the mast in the small boat carried on deck and hoisted the sail on that also.

These ships with their three masts and sails beginning to stretch upwards show the first signs of what was to come in the days of the clipper ships with their towering tiers of sails. But remember that these ships, unlike engine-driven modern ones, were designed to take the hard knocks of the sea on the high poop (see p. 9) more than on the bows.

The round tuck of the early carrack can still be seen, but the deck over the bows is larger and the quarter deck covers nearly half the main deck. Since the steering was still by means of a tiller the steersman had to stand beneath the quarter deck which, with the sails, completely blocked his view.

Since lateen sails were not used on the fore and main masts, the shrouds for these were tightened by deadeyes and lanyards (see p. 12) and were led down to stout small platforms fixed to the outside of the hull.

The ports for the sweeps were still there, but those under the quarter deck were usually for cannon.

Caravels and carrack-type ships led the way, first southwards around Africa and then westwards across the Atlantic. But it was the carrack type with its strength, storage capacity, and steadiness when being driven by winds and waves of the wide ocean that fitted it to be First Around the World.

Much has been made of the first crossing of the Atlantic by Columbus, but his was an easy voyage — easy in comparison with that of Magellan and his men.

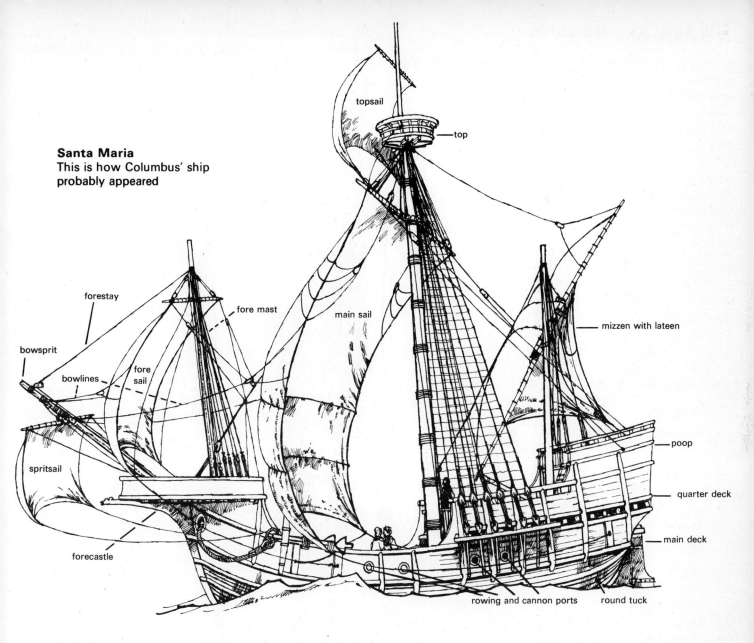

Santa Maria
This is how Columbus' ship probably appeared

topsail

top

forestay

fore mast

main sail

mizzen with lateen

bowsprit

bowlines

fore sail

spritsail

poop

quarter deck

forecastle

main deck

rowing and cannon ports

round tuck

The ship as a machine

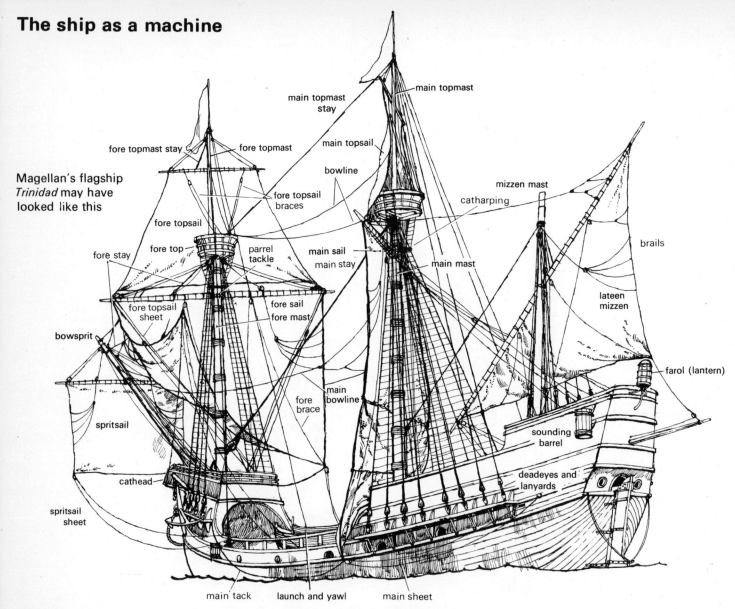

Magellan's flagship *Trinidad* may have looked like this

fore topmast stay

fore topmast

main topmast stay

main topsail

main topmast

bowline

mizzen mast

catharping

fore topsail braces

fore topsail

fore top

parrel tackle

main sail

main stay

main mast

brails

fore stay

main mast

lateen mizzen

fore topsail sheet

fore sail

fore mast

bowsprit

farol (lantern)

fore brace

main bowline

spritsail

sounding barrel

cathead

deadeyes and lanyards

spritsail sheet

main tack

launch and yawl

main sheet

We shall now examine in more detail how the parts of a ship worked together. The hull, the masts, the rigging and the sails were all interlocking sections, forming a complete machine. Each depended on and helped the others. A weakness in one could cause damage elsewhere, or perhaps the total loss of the ship.

We shall take a closer look at one of Magellan's ships. The changes since Columbus' ships will be obvious, but although we are fairly sure how ships generally had developed in those thirty years note carefully that no one knows exactly what any particular one of Magellan's ships looked like. Naturally the main construction was of wood. This meant that though the timbers could be cut and shaped they were liable to rot and wear and also made an excellent home for sea worms. The greatest advantage was that wood swells in water and so the underwater sections tended to hold each other firm and tight. For the same reason sailors never minded a little water slopping around in the bottom of the hold or in the ship's boats – it all helped to make a watertight and safe ship. Wherever possible the plankings were secured by wooden dowels, called treenails, since these would also swell in water and so grip even tighter.

This tendency of wood to swell when wet was one reason why the upper decks were washed down regularly with bucketfuls of salt water – at least once a day, and four or five times a day in the tropics. Without constant soaking the maindeck planking would shrink and crack after a few weeks of dry hot weather.

It was not practical to keep the masts and spars soaked with water so they were rubbed with fish oil and bound at regular intervals with tarred rope.

Masts

The masts passed on the power of the wind from the sails to the hull. The junction of a mast with the hull had to be a strong unmoving union.

The heel, or lowest point, of the mast was set on the keel and supported by cross beams at the main deck. The place where the mast passed through the main deck was the weakest part; it tended to work loose as the mast moved a little when the pressure of the wind changed. Mast wedges were used to make this join tight at all times. Mast wedges were very long tapering pieces of wood usually about $6\frac{1}{2}$ft (2 m) long and about $2\frac{1}{4}$ in (6 cm) wide. These were set up to form a circle around the mast where it entered the deck.

All the vertical masts were secured and steadied in this way, but the bowsprit, which was the smallest mast, entered the ship at an angle. Its heel was secured beneath a heavy baulk of timber on the deck, and where it lay against the fore mast it was lashed. This was the only mast that was not held rigidly – it tended to move up and down and work the lashing loose. This was no great cause for concern since it was such a light mast with a small sail, but nevertheless the lashing needed constant attention.

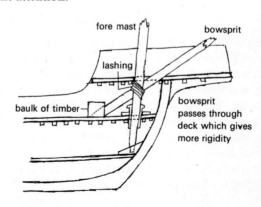

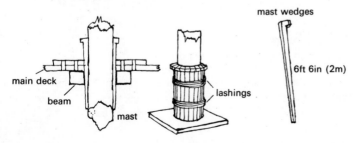

Rigging

Standing rigging

Unless given some further support higher up, the masts would bend and spring like bows – and probably snap. Ropes and tackles were set up to hold them steady against pressure from different directions; this was called standing rigging. All standing rigging was tarred since it was a permanent fixture. However each piece of standing rigging had to be capable of being adjusted a little.

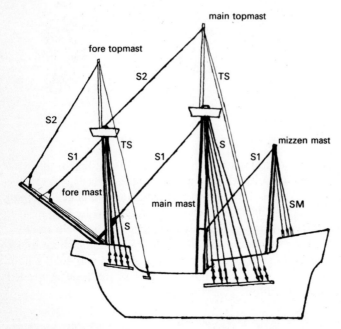

The three masts, fore, main and mizzen, were solid permanent fixtures with their heels set down into the ship. Each mast had a stay leading forward (S1).
The fore and main masts also had shrouds (S) leading to deadeyes, the mizzen had shrouds leading to tackles fastened on deck (S M).
The fore topmast and the main topmast were much lighter and easily replaced or repaired. These had lighter stays (S2) leading forward and lighter shrouds (TS) leading to deadeyes on the ship's side.

Tightening the standing rigging

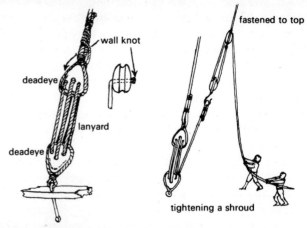

The shrouds on the mizzen were hauled tight by a tackle. All the others were fastened by deadeyes and lanyards. A deadeye was a solid heartshaped block of wood with three holes bored through it. The lower end of each shroud ended in a deadeye and on the ledge outside the bulwarks was another deadeye. A rope called a lanyard was reeved, or passed through, these two deadeyes so that they could be tightened and drawn together.

Reeving and tightening the shrouds was a job for an expert. The tension had to be evenly spread amongst the row of shrouds and the tension on each side of the mast had to be equal. If the shrouds had to be readjusted, then the ratlines, fastened by reef knots, would also be realigned. (Ratlines — see p. 4.)

Cat-harping
Tension in the shrouds could be quickly adjusted at sea by passing a rope around the shrouds and tightly lashing the turns.

Balancing the tension in the shrouds took time and was best done at anchor or in port under the direction of the master. If they had stretched while at sea and the mast was beginning to vibrate a quick temporary method called cat-harping could be used.

The main-mast stay, which ended at the deck, was tightened by deadeyes in the same way as the shrouds. The foremast stay and the main topmast stay ended on the bowsprit and were rigged as shown. The fore and top stays also helped to steady the unstable bowsprit.

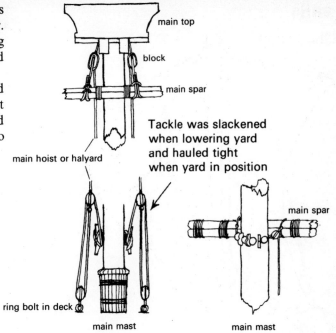

main top

block

main spar

main hoist or halyard

Tackle was slackened when lowering yard and hauled tight when yard in position

ring bolt in deck

main mast

main spar

main mast

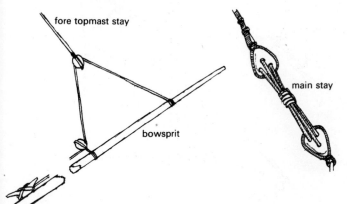

fore topmast stay

bowsprit

main stay

Parrel
Wooden balls and dividers ensured smooth run when yard was lowered

Running rigging

All the other ropes, large and small, which lifted and lowered spars, turned sails, held sails, or were used in the general working of the ship were called running rigging.

One of the most important, and largest, pieces of running rigging was the mainyard hoist. It took most of the weight of the main spar and the main sail.

Two large pulley blocks were slung from the top and two lines led from the spar, through these two blocks, and down to two fixed tackles on the main deck.

The main hoist lifted and lowered the mainyard but it could not hold it against the mast; another device was needed for this, named the parrel.

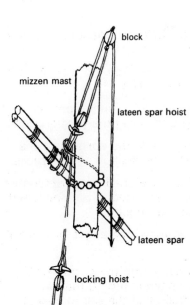

block

mizzen mast

lateen spar hoist

lateen spar

locking hoist

The sails

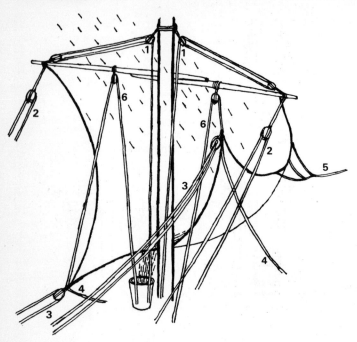

The sails were made of overlapping strips of canvas with a rope edging to strengthen them. At the lower corners the rope was turned into an eye to take the sheet and tack. The arrangement on a lateen sail was of course slightly different but the ropes did very similar jobs to those on a square sail.

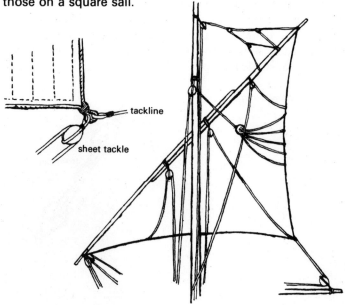

Each sail had a number of ropes to adjust its position, shape and size:

1. *Lifts* Helped to raise the yard, hold its weight and also stop the yard from see-sawing.

2. *Braces* By slacking on one and hauling on the other the braces were used to swing the yard around.

3. *Sheets* The sheet tackles held the corners of the sail back to correspond with the position of the braces.

4. *Tack lines* The tack lines stretched forward, sometimes to the bowsprit, and were used to pull the lower corners of the sail forward as required.

5. *Bowlines* The bowlines pulled the edges of the sail forward when required.

6. *Clew lines* Clew lines hauled up the corner of the sail to the yard and were an aid in furling the sail. They could also make a hollow in the sail to collect rain water.

Fastening the ropes

The ropes of the running rigging had to be fastened in such a way that they could easily be cast loose and altered. So they were twisted around kevels, cleats or belaying pins.

belaying pins, used for light ropes

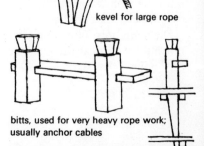

bits, used for very heavy rope work; usually anchor cables

Increasing and decreasing the sail area

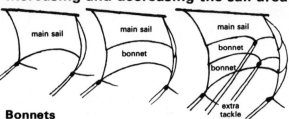

Bonnets

In fair winds extra pieces of sail (bonnets) were attached to the bottom of the main sail. The tackles and lines at the corners had to be moved down to the corner of the bonnet. This made large main sails difficult to control and placed extra strain on the running rigging. To ease this, blocks and tackles were attached to the centre of the sail at the joins of the bonnets.

Lacing of bonnet

This was a continuous lace stitched along the bonnet and forming loops to thread through grommetts in sail.

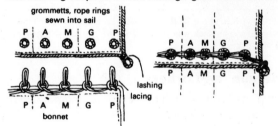

Reefing

Another way of reducing sail area.

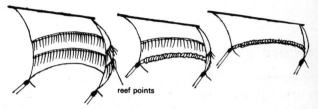

To reduce sail area the sheets and tack lines were unshackled and attached at the lower line of reef points. The spare section of sail was then rolled up and fastened by the reef lines (using a reef knot). To reduce sail area even more the next line of reef points was used.

The letters A.M.G.P. repeated across the width of the sail and bonnet was not just to ensure that the correct loops were pushed through the right grommetts. The sailors repeated what the letters stood for as they laced on the bonnet: 'Ave Maria, Gratia Plena' (Hail Mary, full of grace) – just as if they were reciting the rosary. In a way it was giving thanks for fair winds. Other ships used the letters which spelled out STELLA MARIS (Star of the Sea).

Furling the sails

The safest way to take in a sail was to lower the yard, hauling on the clew lines at the same time. Then, standing on the deck, the sailors could bunch up the sail and lash it to the yard. The whole thing could then be hauled up the mast out of the way.

If the wind was fair and there was no need to lower the yard the sailors had to climb aloft and sit astride the yard. They shuffled themselves along, while below someone heaved on the clew lines. The sail was hauled up by hand and lashed to the yard. This required a good sense of balance for there were no footropes such as later ships had.

When the spritsail was furled, the yard was laid alongside the bowsprit and lashed there.

Thus the power of the wind was transferred through the sails, masts, and standing and running rigging, into the hull.

There was, however, a limit to the strength of the equipment. Great care had to be taken to adjust the sail spread to the force of the wind — otherwise sails would tear, masts would snap, or else the planking of the hull would be strained and the seams opened. The greatest danger came from being caught unawares by a sudden squall. In such emergencies the sails were released to fly loose or the yards quickly dropped to the deck.

The whole ship was an intricate machine, each small section playing its part. As a working unit it creaked and groaned as it plowed its way over the seas.

MAGELLAN'S VOYAGE: THE ATLANTIC

Officers and men

In the summer of 1519, in Seville, the crews for Magellan's ships were signed on. The crew lists show that they came not only from San Lucar, the out-port for Seville, but from Portugal, France, Greece, Genoa and Germany. The voyage was under Royal Charter and was expected to last two years, sailing westwards to the Spice Islands, and for those who signed on there was six months' pay in advance.

The Portuguese, wanting no interference with their monopoly of the oceanic spice trade, did their best to sabotage the proceedings by spreading false rumours and hindering the loading of the vessels. Their efforts were in vain. Magellan had an excellent reputation as an officer who looked after his men and many believed he held a secret chart showing a passage through the Americas into the Southern Ocean.

Magellan could pick his men. Two hundred and thirty-four were chosen. They were divided among the five ships:

SHIP	CAPACITY	CAPTAIN	MASTER	CREW
Trinidad*	110 tons	Ferdinand Magellan (Captain-General)	Esteban Gomez (PILOT: Juan de Punzarol)	55 men
San Antonio	120 tons	Juan de Cartagena	Juan de Eloriaga	60 men
Concepcion	90 tons	Gaspar de Quesada	Juan Sebastian de Elcano	45 men
Victoria	85 tons	Luis de Mendoza	Anton Salmon	42 men
Santiago	75 tons	Juan de Serrano	Ballasar	32 men

*Magellan's flagship, about 80 ft (25 metres) long and 25 ft (7.5 metres) wide at the waterline. The deck was about 22 ft (6.7 metres) and its loaded draft 9 ft (2.6 metres).

'Gentlemen' and others

A normal working merchant ship was commanded by a Master, who had probably worked his way up from deck boy (nicknamed a 'grommet'). The crew could question his decisions and, if all agreed, could countermand his orders. He only held command because the crew respected his experience and seamanship. But when a ship was under Royal Authority the situation changed. The 'Gentlemen', or 'Hidalgos', arrived.

To be an Hidalgo was to be of distinguished birth and breeding. No one argued with an Hidalgo – except another Hidalgo. To everyday folk they were a race apart – to be bowed before and obeyed.

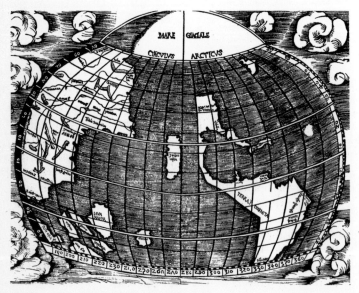

◄A woodcut map made by Martin Waldseemuller in 1507. He made a good guess at the continuous coastline of North and South America but showed Japan as a large island only 10° West of the American coast.

Each ship of the Magellan expedition received an Hidalgo as its Captain. Between the Captain and the crew was an impassable barrier. He not only gave orders through the Master alone but he carried a letter of Royal Authority and held the power of life and death over the sailors. The full complement of one of the ships would have been something like this:

Gentlemen (Hidalgos)

Captain	In full command but he did not need to know the technicalities of navigation or ship handling.
Supernumeraries	Three was a common number to carry but it varied considerably. They were extra to the crew and were social companions for the Captain. The best example is that of Antonio Pigafetta, an Italian gentleman, who sailed with Magellan purely out of interest and who wrote a complete record of the voyage.

These Hidalgos formed a select group known as the Afterguard.

The Rest

Master	In charge of the running of the ship and adviser to the Captain.
Pilot	In charge of all aspects of navigation, usually providing his own charts, instruments, lode stone and sounding lead.
Clerk	Secretary to the Captain and responsible for keeping a complete record of all cargo collected.
Priest	Spiritual adviser for the whole crew. His duties could be performed by the Captain if no priest was carried.

These were allowed to join the Captain at meal times and so were sometimes classed as part of the Afterguard. A priest or secretary might in any case be a gentleman.

The senior mariners	They were on a footing not much below the Master, and the boatswain (bosun) was quite capable of running the ship.
Boatswain	Responsible to the Master for the working of the ship and crew.
Surgeon	He provided his own instruments and medicines.
Master at Arms	Responsible to the Captain for the discipline on board. He punished offenders and also trained the crew as a fighting unit. All armament and powder were under his control.
Carpenter	In a completely wooden ship his importance is obvious. He brought his own tools.
Caulker	Of equal importance to the carpenter; responsible for the watertightness of the vessel.
Boatswain's mate	A very experienced sailor who assisted the boatswain.
Gentlemen's steward and cook	In charge of all foodstuffs, and the cooking of meals.
Assistant stewards	Two in number.
Master gunner	Experienced in handling cannon.
Gunners	Two in number.

Mariners	General seamen who were also specialists. They were invaluable members of the crew and were capable of taking over as boatswain or boatswain's mate. About six in number. They specialised thus: a cooper who made and repaired casks and barrels; a tailor; painter and paint mixer; barber; Master helmsman. It is possible that all the mariners were Master helmsmen.

(No crew lists of this period mention a sailmaker—a vital task. It seems likely that all mariners had to be capable of making and repairing sails.)

Leading seamen	Seven in number. Young sailors with a few years experience.
Apprentice seamen	Four in number.
Ship's boys	Youngsters who were 'general dog's-bodies' for the Master, priest, pilot and clerk. Two in number.
Pages	Pages for the Hidalgos. Two in number. These may have considered themselves as part of the Afterguard.

This would give a total of 41, rather less than Magellan's fleet, and we shall imagine this as our typical crew.

Pay

The Master and pilot received about 2000 maravedis a month, the senior mariners 1500, mariners 1000, leading seamen 800, and ship's boys 666 a month.

It is difficult to give modern values but a comparison with other prices at the time will give you some idea: a cow would cost 2000 maravedis, a pig 400 and a duck 35.

Guns, stores and cargo

We are lucky to have a list of the stores and cargo taken aboard Magellan's fleet. It was made by a man called Martin Fernandez de Navarrete. It is as follows:

Weapons

58 large cannon. (Probably firing a 10 lb ball)
   14 to the *Trinidad*
   12 to the *San Antonio*
   12 to the *Concepcion*
   12 to the *Victoria*
    8 to the *Santiago*
7 falconets (small cannon)
3 large bombards and three small ones
5000 lbs of gunpowder
Cannon balls of lead and stone
50 arquebuses with tripods
60 crossbows
369 dozen arrows
95 dozen darts
10 dozen javelins
1000 lances
200 pikes
60 boarding pikes

Armour

100 mail corselets with armlets and shoulder plates
100 breastplates with throat pieces
100 helmets
200 shields
For the use of the Captain-General: a coat of mail, two suits of armour and six sword blades.

Food

15 tons ship's biscuits in barrels
6100 lbs in barrels of beans, lentils and peas
5700 lbs dried pork
984 cheeses
1512 lbs of honey in jars
16 casks of figs
3200 lbs of raisins, currants and almonds

322 lbs of rice
100 lbs of mustard
5 pipes of fine flour (a pipe will hold 105 gallons)
5600 lbs of vinegar
450 strings of garlic and onions
(Though not recorded, there would be casks of water and wine, olive oil, dried fish, other salted meats, salt, herbs and numerous live pigs and hens in coops. The livestock would be killed at sea.)

Stores

Spare casks, mats, baskets and barrels
2 fishing nets, harpoons, fish spears, 10,500 fish hooks
40 cartloads of wood
Spare planking and spars lashed on deck
417 pipes and 253 wine butts
15 padlocks
15 books for accounts
42 pint measures
6 cauldrons
6 pots
Two ovens for shore use
Kettles for melting pitch
A forge with bellows
Anvil
Blacksmith's tools
Grindstone
12 pairs of bellows for galley
Scales and balances plus weights

Tools

(Rope splicing equipment, mallets etc.)
Cordage, spare canvas, blocks, oars, boat hooks, pumpleather and leather for chafing gear, nails

89 small lanterns and two large ship's lanterns
100 mess bowls
200 porringers
100 choppers
66 wooden platters
94 trenchers
80 flags, Royal Standard
5 drums, brass horns, bugles and 20 tambourines
Small hand guns
Manacles and leg irons
Candles for religious services

In the holds would be stowed the goods to be used for trading for the spices:
1 ton quicksilver
1½ tons vermilion
5 tons alum
30 pieces coloured cloth
20 lbs saffron
3 pieces very fine fabric
8 pieces Valencia stuff
8 pieces coloured velvet
50 pieces of buckram
20,000 lbs lump copper
10,000 lbs lead
some combs
400 doz. cheap knives
500 lbs crystals
10,000 fish hooks
200 red caps
200 gaudy handkerchiefs
4000 brass and copper bracelets
20,000 small bells

The list of supplies shows what appears to be a large number of guns and other weapons – but it was always possible that seamen would have to fight for their lives, or for food, against hostile natives. The Captains also knew that if they ever met with Portuguese vessels there was sure to be a battle. In fact a Portuguese fleet was already preparing to waylay Magellan in the Atlantic and to destroy the whole expedition.

Previous drawings have shown three cannon on each side, but this is only a guess. The *San Antonio* had 12 cannon. But it is unlikely that all twelve were carried on the main deck since this could make the ship unstable. It is more probable that six were on deck ready for use while the rest were stowed in the hold to be used ashore or in emergencies. These guns were lashed into wooden cradles which were in turn lashed to rings in the deck and bulwark. The inboard end was not tied to the deck and a wedge was inserted here to lower or raise the barrel, but it was not turned sideways – the ship had to turn to aim the gun. A row of preloaded chambers was kept ready; they were fired by placing a hot iron or wadding (i.e. specially prepared cord) match to the touch hole. The ammunition could be varied from iron or stone balls to bucketfulls of small shot or stones.

Each ship would also have one or two falconets (4.5 cm calibre). These were swivel guns that were portable and could be fixed on to supports along the gunwales.

Under lock in the Captain's cabin were a number of small hand guns. These were simply muzzle loaded tubes attached to wooden stocks. One was held in the left hand while the right hand applied the wadding match to the touch hole.

Any one of these guns could be fired, without ammunition, as a sound signal, but a preloaded chamber was easier to use. It was hung from some support, like those that held the falconets, and then fired.

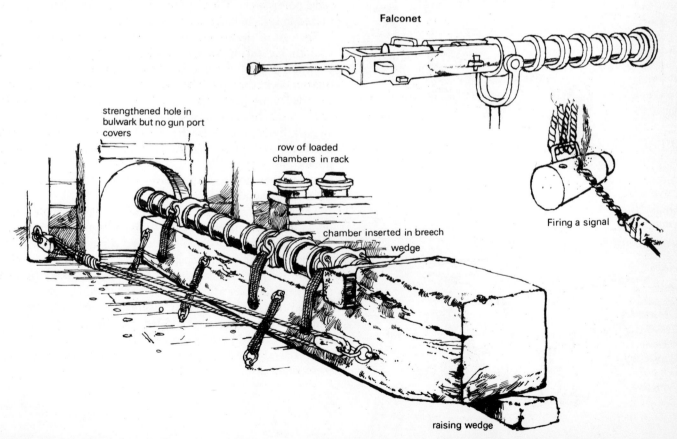

Falconet

strengthened hole in bulwark but no gun port covers

row of loaded chambers in rack

chamber inserted in breech

wedge

Firing a signal

raising wedge

Section along centre of ship

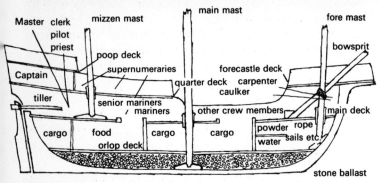

Labels: Master, clerk, pilot, priest; mizzen mast; main mast; fore mast; poop deck; supernumeraries; bowsprit; Captain; forecastle deck; quarter deck; carpenter; caulker; tiller; senior mariners; mariners; other crew members; main deck; cargo; food; cargo; cargo; powder; rope; water; sails etc.; orlop deck; stone ballast

Plan of main deck

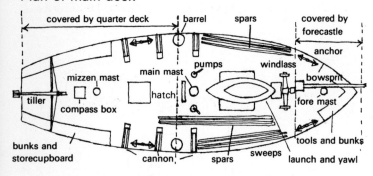

Labels: covered by quarter deck; barrel; spars; covered by forecastle; anchor; pumps; windlass; mizzen mast; main mast; bowsprit; tiller; hatch; fore mast; compass box; bunks and storecupboard; cannon; spars; sweeps; tools and bunks; launch and yawl

Home for four

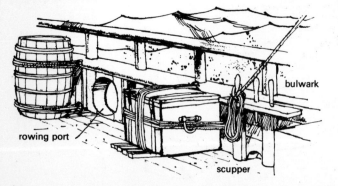

Labels: bulwark; rowing port; scupper

Loading the ships

During the summer months of 1519 cartload after cartload rolled along the wooden quays of Seville until the whole list of stores and cargo had been checked and the masses of equipment stowed away on board the ships. The cargo and stores would be passed down through the hatches and stowed between the main deck and orlop deck – in the hold. The space beneath the orlop deck held the stones used to ballast the ship.

Only one person, the Captain, had a cabin to himself. The rest had to find space on the main deck. Some of the supernumeraries and page boys may have been allowed on the quarter deck; in front of the Captain's cabin.

Naturally the amount of personal belongings that a crew member could take on the voyage had to be limited. Expeditions under Royal Commission followed a general pattern. The chest size was regulated to nothing larger than '5 palms long and 3 palms high'. The Captain could bring one chest which he placed in his small cabin on the quarter deck.

The rest of the crew could have, or share, chests. With the Captain's chest in the quarter-deck cabin, and perhaps the communal chest of the ship's boys and pages stowed on the quarter deck, there were 20 chests to be stowed on the already crowded main deck. This main deck was cluttered with the tiller, masts, compass box, ladders, spare anchors, spare yards, sweeps, hatches, barrels, the launch, the yawl, bilge pumps, livestock, and all the rigging leading to cleats and belaying points. Amongst all this, nearly 40 men had to find a space that would be their home for two years – and yet not be in the way of the normal running of the ship.

The carpenter, caulker and gunners would probably settle under the forecastle where their tools and equipment would be stowed in long low lockers that could serve as bunks. Under the shelter of the quarter deck the senior mariners would settle. The Master, clerk, pilot and priest would be likely to claim space near the tiller where wooden bunks could be built against the bulwarks. The boatswain, surgeon and master-at-arms would settle near the open end but still under shelter. The rest of the crew could use any space left; some might manage to get under the quarter deck but most would have to be content with the open deck.

The Fleet departs

Monday 10 August 1519

In the morning crowds of sightseers and the relatives of the crews watched the procession winding its colourful way from the church down to the quays where the ships' launches waited. The Captains in their fine cloaks and silken clothes led the seamen through the streets. Leading all went the Royal Standard and then came the Captain-General himself, a knight of the order of Santiago with the cross of St James emblazoned on his tabard. The final act of preparation was over. Each seaman had made confession and taken communion, and the ships and standards had been blessed.

The fleet had been moved to midstream and now, with sails furled, swinging gently at anchor, the yellow-hulled vessels seemed asleep. Then as the crews clambered up the sides all turned to activity. Windlasses creaked and the anchor ropes crawled aboard. The riggings were dotted with the red and blue bonnets of the seamen and the sails flopped down, shook for a moment, and then billowed out.

From the shore cannon fired salutes and the fleet gathered way. Never again would the ships look as they looked now. Long pennants and standards snaked from mast and yard, the paintwork gleamed, splendidly blazoned shields were ranged along the bulwarks, and the Hidalgos waved their plumed hats.

Once the ships were out of sight of Seville an order was given. Within an hour the finery was gone. Flags, banners and shields disappeared, rich clothes were carefully packed away. The display was over – the work had begun.

At San Lucar, in sight of the Atlantic, the fleet anchored and set about final preparations. Movable objects were stowed away or lashed down, compasses and charts checked and last minute stores were ordered. All this took time and after waiting for favourable winds it was not until Tuesday 20 September that the ships weighed anchor and headed south-west into blue water.

The river front at Seville. From a late sixteenth-century painting.

Weighing the anchor

Twenty or so men held the cable and walked aft. On reaching the tiller area, the end man let go and ran forward to take up the cable again. Others passed the cable down the forward hatch.

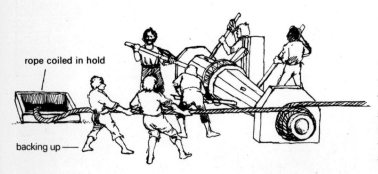

rope coiled in hold

backing up

If there was any strain on the cable then the windlass was used. A few turns of the cable were passed around the windlass end and backed up by two or three seamen. (Backing up means leaning back while holding the cable). Others would use the windlass bars to turn the windlass. A simple ratchet prevented it from running back.

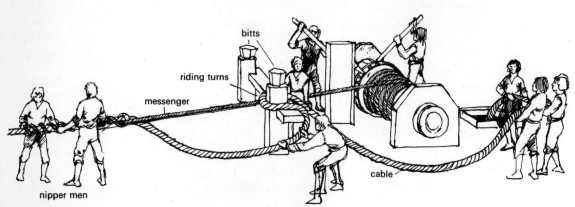

bitts

riding turns

messenger

nipper men

cable

In large ships the anchor was very heavy and the cable correspondingly thicker, so thick that it could not be turned on the barrel of the windlass. In such cases a messenger was used. A messenger is a rope that transfers power.

While the ship was being heaved along to a position above the anchor the work was not unduly hard. It was when the cable was vertical and held the weight of the anchor that the greatest strain was felt.

If by any chance the windlass was out of order then a tackle could be used, with stoppers to take the strain during change overs.

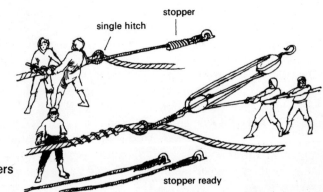

single hitch

stopper

stopper ready

Catting the anchor

By the time the anchor was clear of the water the ship was well under way, but the work with the anchor was not finished. If it was not made fast it could stave in the ship's bows. The diagram below shows what was done.

(1) Two blocks of solid timber projected from the bows, one on each side. These were called catheads. (2) A tackle hung down from the cathead and an agile sailor hooked the end of the tackle into the ring of the anchor. (3) On deck the crew heaved on the tackle and took the weight of the anchor. (4) The anchor was heaved up tight to the cathead and lashed firmly by the ring. Meanwhile a seaman was 'fishing' for one of the flukes with a rope with an eyesplice in it. Once the fluke was hooked it was heaved to the ship's side and lashed there.

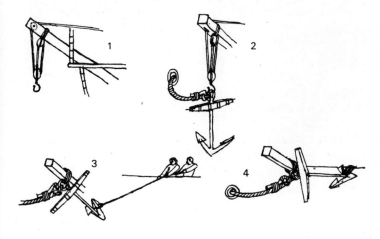

Daily routine

With the anchors stowed, the fleet was now heading for Tenerife in the Canary Islands and the normal routine of life at sea could begin. Watches were set.

The days at sea were divided into three parts, called watches. The crew were divided into three groups and each group was appointed to a watch. During the eight hours of each watch the seamen were working, or standing by ready to obey orders, or on tiller duty, or on lookout duty. When off watch they were free to attend to their own affairs, except for regular deck washing, church services or emergencies. Some system of change ensured that each seaman had a turn at each watch – the second

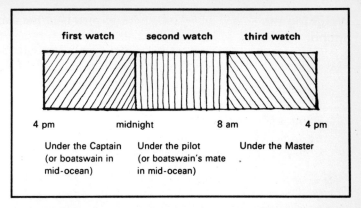

first watch	second watch	third watch
Under the Captain (or boatswain in mid-ocean)	Under the pilot (or boatswain's mate in mid-ocean)	Under the Master

4 pm — midnight — 8 am — 4 pm

watch being most desirable since it was the easiest, though perhaps boring.

The watches were timed by a half-hour sand glass which stood beside the compass. A duty boy had to stand watch on the glass and turn it over as soon as the sand ran out. During the boring night hours it was tempting to 'warm' the glass. This was done by placing the hands around the glass and letting the body heat warm it, which made the sand run faster and thus speed the passage of the watch. However, this was punishable by a severe flogging – it was rarely attempted.

When the duty boy turned the glass during the night he called out:

'One glass is gone and now the second floweth
All shall run down, if God willeth.
To my God let us pray, let us good voyage,
And through his blessed mother, our advocate on high,
Protect us from the water spout and send no tempest nigh.'

If it was the sixth glass the first line would be:

'Six glasses have gone and now the seventh floweth'.

In this way the duty boy was a 'talking clock' for the whole ship.

A boy walked around the main deck just before the ending of his watch and called:

'On deck – on deck, gentlemen mariners of the second watch.
On deck in good time.
You are Mister Pilot's watch.
For it is duty time – shake a leg.'

The setting and rising of the sun were always marked by special prayers.

The most popular prayer was the one that signalled the ending of the watch. As the seventh hour passed the prayer went:

'Good is that which passeth.
Better that which cometh.
Seven is past and eight floweth.
More shall flow if God willeth.
Count and pass – make voyage fast.'

Special services and masses were held on Saturday and Sunday. The whole crew assembled on the main deck before an altar set up on seachests and the service was led by the Captain and priest with boys acting as acolytes.

Lookouts were on duty at all times and during the night on each hour a call was made to them:

'Hey – you – forward. Look alive.
    keep good watch.'

The lookout had to reply 'Good Watch', just to prove he was awake.

Food

We have noted earlier the type of food loaded. In theory these stores were intended to last out the voyage, but much of the food was unable to stand the long storage in the damp holds. But it could not be wasted. Biscuits issued during day time were often kept until nightfall – when they ate them in the darkness the crew did not have to look at the maggots that crawled in the biscuits.

The food store was well locked and water was strictly rationed. Fishing for extra food over the side of the ship went on at all times and whenever shore was reached the first thought was always to send men in search of food and water.

About eleven in the morning the only hot meal of the day was served. The food was cooked on a portable kitchen unit which was usually set up on the main deck. If the weather was bad and seas were being shipped over the rail the unit could be moved until it was just under the shelter of the quarter deck. In violent storms no hot meals were prepared.

The portable kitchen was simply a large three sided iron box about a metre high with a layer of sand and earth in the bottom.

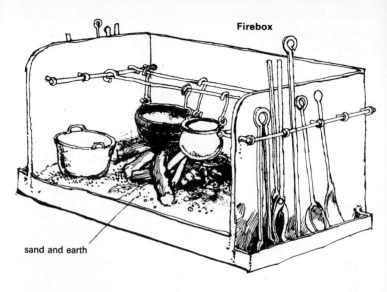

Firebox

sand and earth

Firewood was burned on the sand, and extra buckets of sand and sea water were placed nearby in case the ship's deck should catch fire.

For the benefit of the Afterguard a table was set up on the quarter deck. This table was often simply chests pushed together, with the gentlemen sitting on low stools. The meals for this group had to be announced in the correct manner. One of the apprentices called out in a loud voice:

'Table, table, Sir Captain and Master and good company.
Food is ready — water as usual — for Sir Captain,
    Master and good company.
Long live the King of Castile by land and sea.
Who says to him war — off with his head.
Who won't say Amen — gets nothing to drink.
Table is set — who won't come to eat?'

For the rest of the crew the affair was much simpler. They lined up at the firebox. Each seaman carried his own wooden trough and spoon, a plate, an earthenware soup bowl, an eating knife and a drinking horn for water or wine. Once served they carried their food to some convenient and comfortable spot and sat down to eat it. A boy walked around with a leather bottle of wine and poured a small amount for each man.

Across the Atlantic

After a good trip the fleet put into Tenerife on 26 September, taking on extra food and water. Magellan received a letter warning him of the Portuguese fleet awaiting him, so on 3 October he sailed south to the seas off Sierra Leone and so dodged the ambush. There he took advantage of the south-east trade winds and headed for the coast of Brazil.

Some of his Captains, perhaps jealous of his position, questioned his course and caused trouble. One Captain, Juan de Cartagena, was removed from command and placed in stocks on the forecastle of the *Trinidad*. On the whole it was difficult for the Captains to argue with Magellan. They had to bring their ships close to the *Trinidad* and bawl their objections across the water. Magellan could choose not to answer or else reply, 'Follow my flag by day — and my lantern by night.'

Formation at sea

General sailing orders were usually given before the voyage started. After that it was simply a matter of 'do as I do'.

During the hours of daylight this was fairly simple. When the flagship shortened sail, so did the others. When she altered course, so did the others. A period of heavy squalls and storms might separate the fleet. When things calmed down it was up to the others to search around until they found the flagship.

The hours of darkness posed a problem, but Magellan's orders were laid down very clearly. On the stern of the flagship was to be fixed the farol, an iron-framed lantern. The farol was a sign of command, and no other ship but the flagship could carry one. Inside the lantern, shielded by thin sheets of mica, were two or three large wax candles, giving a bright pin-point of light. To give a more glaring and stronger light, firewood could be burned inside the iron frame. Straggling astern, the other ships could follow the single light through the darkest of nights.

Night signals

Magellan had to know if his fleet was there, so at odd intervals another light was set beside the farol light. This was a signal that all ships had to show a single light. Magellan simply looked astern and counted the lights. All these other signal lights were made by setting alight a trenche. This

Punta de Hidalgo, Tenerife (Canary Islands)

was a thick cord of dried reeds. Magellan had a simple signal code for the most likely orders. After the flagship had made the signal, each ship had to repeat it to show that the order had been understood.

Two lights Watch me closely for signals – I am changing my tack, or reducing speed, or something else due to change in weather.
Three lights Remove bonnet. (Usually so that the mainsail could be lowered quickly in a squall.)
Three lights Replace bonnet.
Four lights Lower sails.
Single light (after four lights). Stop and turn.
Four lights (when stopped). Make sail.
Ship ablaze with as many lights as possible – cannons fired – crew shouting. EMERGENCY, or shoal immediately ahead. The only way for complicated orders to be passed was for the whole fleet to heave to. All sails except the mizzen were taken in, the ships would swing into the wind and be held there. Yawls were lowered and the respective Captains rowed across to the flagship.

Finding the way

Possible arrangement of ship's compass and accessories

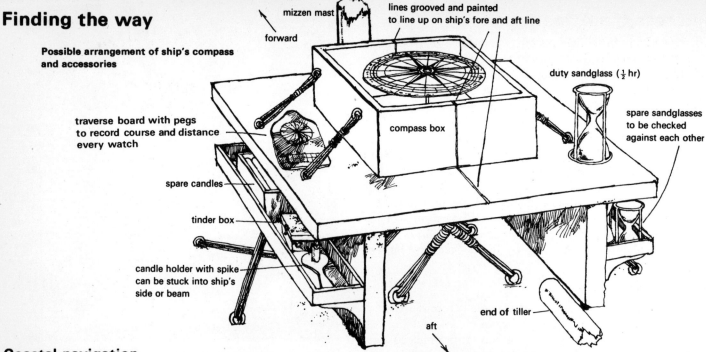

- mizzen mast
- forward
- lines grooved and painted to line up on ship's fore and aft line
- duty sandglass (½ hr)
- spare sandglasses to be checked against each other
- compass box
- traverse board with pegs to record course and distance every watch
- spare candles
- tinder box
- candle holder with spike can be stuck into ship's side or beam
- end of tiller
- aft

Coastal navigation

Navigation along known coasts was a simple and reasonably safe affair. The pilot knew exactly where he was starting from, where he was going, and what to expect on the way. The main worry was that of being driven on to a lee shore. A lee shore is the dangerous situation when a sailing ship cannot make headway against the wind which is blowing directly towards a nearby coast.

When Magellan's fleet approached a new, and hence unknown, shore, caution was always the key word. Ships anchored for the night, or, if that was impossible, turned round and sailed slowly back on their original course until dawn. Lookouts were on constant watch and the leadsman regularly checked the depth of water. Anyone who could speak a little of the languages of the East was welcomed as a crew member and such men were expected to gather sailing directions from the local inhabitants.

The direction finder

Once out of sight of land and in cloudy weather when sun and stars were obscured, the only thing that could show in what direction they were heading was the compass. This was a large magnetised needle fastened to the underside of a circular card. The whole was pivoted on a fine brass point so that it could swing freely. The compass was housed in a small open-topped box which was illuminated at night either by a lantern hanging from the beam above or by a candle in a recess in the box. This box was probably lashed firmly on to a solid table, which in turn was fixed to the deck in front of the tillerman. This arrangement is only a guess — some say that the compass was housed in a small cupboard-like box, the bittacle. The ship's direction, or course, was the point on the compass card that was in line with the painted line inside the box.

Only the pilot was allowed to handle the compass. He carried spare needles — Magellan himself carried 35 of them — and a lodestone. The lodestone was his most prized possession and was guarded carefully. This piece of naturally magnetic stone was stroked across the compass needle to re-magnetise it.

Since the ships were made of wood, there was no local magnetic field to blanket the earth's pull on the magnetic needle. The sailors knew enough to make sure that swords or other large metal objects were never placed near the compass.

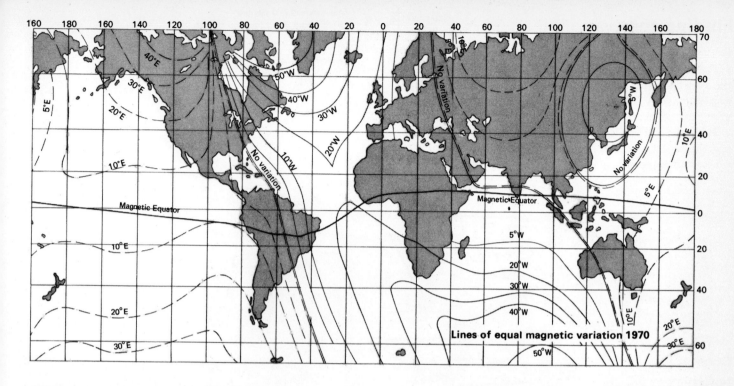

Lines of equal magnetic variation 1970

The accuracy of the compass

Compasses do not point to the geographic north but to the magnetic north. The difference between the two, called 'variation', is different at different places on earth and at different times. Today, variation differs from 20 degrees East in the Straits of Magellan to 30 degrees West off the Cape of Good Hope.

The *reason* for variation may not have been understood in Magellan's day, but sailors did know of its existence. It caused no concern, since the amount of variation could always be found by comparing the bearing of the North Star, or Pole star, with the compass North or by observing the rising of the constellation Orion's Belt, in which the central stars are due east and west.

When making a rough check on variation, the pilot brought the compass on deck and placed it before him in line with the Pole star. He raised his right hand to sight the star, then brought it down vertically to the rim of the compass box. When doing this, he looked as if he were blessing the compass. In fact, this action was often known as 'the pilot's blessing'.

Small errors such as a badly mounted card or a non-central pivot point might exist and go unnoticed. At sea the compass swung as the ship corkscrewed along, and the only way to check the compass with any reasonable accuracy was to take it ashore and test it there. This the pilots did whenever time and conditions permitted.

Finding variation by the North Star

12°   no error   15°

variation
12° West

variation
15° East

27

Steering

Back under the shadow of the quarter deck the helmsman was cut off from the rest of the ship. Even the view forward through the open end of his cave-like area was blocked by the base of the mizzen mast. A ladder leading up through a hatch in the deck above cut off even more of his view.

From the quarter deck above him, orders were shouted down and the expert tillerman had to steer the ship by the feel of the tiller and the movement of the ship beneath his feet.

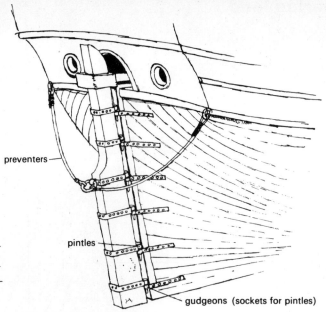

preventers

pintles

gudgeons (sockets for pintles)

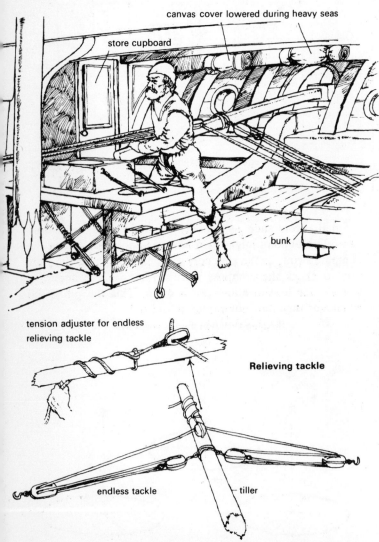

canvas cover lowered during heavy seas

store cupboard

bunk

tension adjuster for endless relieving tackle

Relieving tackle

endless tackle

tiller

The ships were designed to sail with the wind aft. This meant that as the wind increased so did the action of the waves on the stern. As the swell shortened the rudder would be immersed one second, then would be suddenly thrust three quarters of its length into the air. Waves riding on the swell would break against the rudder giving it from time to time savage side jolts. An inexperienced tillerman could receive a nasty blow from the tiller and be sent headlong across the deck. To take the force out of such jolts and to keep a lively tiller under control a 'damping' system of blocks and tackles was set up. As the force of the seas increased so the tillerman controlled the pressure of the relieving tackle by moving the single block along the tiller shaft.

Other rope preventers outside the hull stopped the rudder turning more than about 60 degrees and also held on to it if it was jolted out of its gudgeons.

Nearing land

leadsman

sounding barrel

Eyes, nose and tongue

Naturally the eyes of the lookout were vital at all times. He was not only looking for land but also for signs of land – weed, drifting wood, types of birds and their movements, the colour of the sea, and cloud formations. But not only eyes were used. On deck bucketfuls of sea water were drawn up and tasted for brackishness, and a sensitive nose was sniffing away for any hint of land.

A lump of lead attached to a line was the only 'eye' that could see beneath the ship and tell how much water lay beneath the hull. A high lookout could sometimes see shoal water ahead but the only sure way was to take soundings. The depth could be checked from any position along the ship's side but normally soundings were taken from the poop.

The leadsman stood in a barrel that was lashed to the ship's side. This way he overhung the side and could swing his lead-line without obstruction. When the ship was stationary the line was simply lowered and dumped up and down to make sure the lead was touching the bottom. When under way the leadsman swung the lead back and forth on a long length of line. As it swung up and towards the bows he let go, letting the line run out from the coil in his other hand. As the ship moved over the lead he took in the slack and 'dumped' when the line was vertical.

There was no standard way of marking the line for depth but it may have been marked in brazos (arm lengths) which were nearly the same as fathoms (6 ft.).

When entering a strange harbour or channel the leadsman would be rowed ahead of the ship in a small boat, taking soundings as he went, and so would guide his ship through safe waters.

There was a hollow in the bottom of the lead which was filled with tallow. After a sounding, any sand or mud picked up by the tallow was examined for texture, colour, and was tasted and smelt. Many seamen, in their home waters, could navigate in fog by taste and smell.

lead armed with tallow

tallow

Launching the ship's boats

The ship's launch was a heavy, solid, working boat about 27 feet (8 m) long and over 6 feet (2 m) wide at its broadest. It was usually reckoned that 50 launch-loads of cargo would fill the ship's holds. It was stowed upright in the centre of the main-deck and held oars and a sail of its own.

Placed on top of this was the ship's yawl, or small boat, which was used for general light work and for carrying Hidalgos from ship to ship. The yawl was about 15 feet (4 or 5 m) long and also carried a sail and oars. The sails of these boats could be hoisted to add to the sail power of the ship during light winds.

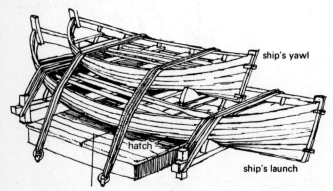

A good spot to stow a chest
or sleep when crossing the ocean

When not in use the sails were stowed in waxed canvas bags to prevent them getting wet and so rotting. The boats themselves were not covered since it was not desirable for the wood to dry and shrink. A foot of water in the boat was preferable to none at all and it was easy to drain out water before using the boat. Lifting these boats, especially the launch, into the sea was a heavy task and could not be performed when the ship was under way with the sails spread. The ship's sails had to be furled, lashings on the yawl released, and lifting tackles fastened to the ends of the main yards of the fore and main masts.

To the edge of the unknown

The fleet made the Atlantic crossing safely, meeting only one bad storm on the way. Their landfall was Cape Roque in Brazil, but Magellan kept well clear of the land. All of South America to the east of the Line of Demarcation was officially Portuguese territory, so the fleet moved south until they seemed well clear of all signs of the Portuguese. On 13 December 1519 they anchored in the beautiful harbour which we now call Rio de Janeiro. Rio de Janeiro proved to be an excellent choice. It had a sheltered harbour, plenty of food and water, and very friendly natives. The crew found some profitable bargains — one fish hook or a playing card could be swapped for six chickens. Hamacas (hammocks) were seen by many for the first time, but we have no record of any enterprising seaman who tried one out on board ship.

They left Rio on 13 December and followed the coastline south-westwards.

MAGELLAN'S VOYAGE: THE PACIFIC

Latitude 34½° S

The discovery of a large river estuary in January 1520 proved that they were now at the limits of all previous exploration. Juan de Solis had been killed and eaten by natives hereabouts four years ago and his ship had turned back. Magellan called the river Rio de Solis in honour of the man who had died there. (Later Sebastian Cabot renamed it Rio de la Plata or River of Silver.)

The fleet now moved on – into completely unknown waters.

A pause for rest

From henceforth all knew that any land they saw had never before been seen by a European. During February and March the ships edged cautiously southwards, hugging the coast, seeking any hint of a channel leading westwards.

Two islands were discovered and some very strange creatures were found. The islands were covered with geese which showed no fear of man. They were black, could not fly and had the beak of a crow. Hundreds were slaughtered for food and it was found that the birds could not be plucked but had to be skinned. There were also seawolves with heads like a calf and webbed nails at their sides.

The southern winter was closing in. Icy winds were blowing and the hours of darkness were growing longer. On 31 March 1520 a sheltered bay with sandy beaches was found and the fleet drew in and decided to settle down for the winter. Magellan named it St Julian's Bay. It was in 49½° South, and the ships dropped anchor in calm and protected waters.

A 'goose' and a 'seawolf'.

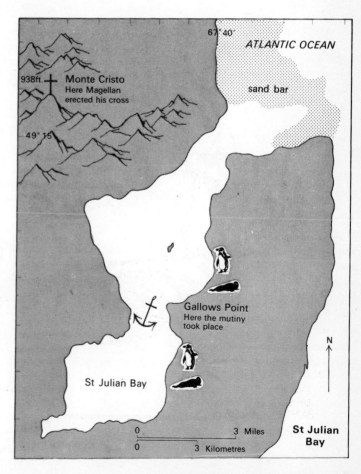

Anchoring

When preparing to anchor all lashings were removed in reverse order to that in which they were put on, and the anchor hung down on its cable. The weight was taken by a stopper. Enough cable to cover the depth of water was flaked out on deck, then a riding turn was taken on the bitts (see p. 22).

On the order the stopper was released — if it jammed an axe was always ready to sever the stopper. The anchor dragged the cable until it struck the bottom. As the ship slowly swung to the tide or wind the men at the bitts eased the turns and so passed out the cable.

The stopper man was in a dangerous position. Once he had released the stopper he had to leap to safety as the cable lashed around on its way to the hawse hole.

When the Master decided that enough cable had been paid out, the order to make fast was given and extra turns were taken around the bitts. Using two anchors at the bow had a disadvantage. The ship still swung around to tide and wind, and the cables could get crossed and twisted. To clear such 'fouled' anchors the crew had to man the launch and tow the ship around until all was clear. Where a ship was expected to turn to the tide and it was desirable to hold the ship stationary, then stern anchors as well as bow anchors were used.

It was not always necessary to move the ship in order to put out another anchor. The ship's launch could be used to carry it to its position. The anchor was lowered into the water and lashings passed through its ring and around the launch. The

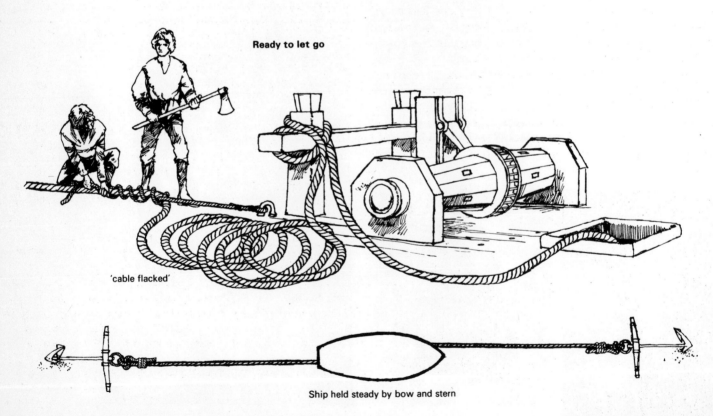

Ready to let go

'cable flacked'

Ship held steady by bow and stern

launch was rowed with the anchor slung beneath and the lashings passed over baulks of timber laid across the point of balance. When the launch was in position the lashings were severed with an axe. Another aid when anchored in narrow waters or confined harbours was to attach a line to the ring of the anchor before letting go. Later, when it was required to swing the ship, this line was heaved upon.

If bad weather made the anchor drag then more anchors were dropped. If things got really bad then large heavy objects were 'frapped' to the cable. A ship often carried up to eleven anchors. Four bow anchors, four stern anchors, a stream anchor (used at sea to keep head into swell), a kedge anchor (used for hauling the ship up rivers or through shoal water), and a large sheet anchor. The sheet anchor, stowed upright beside the mast in the hold, was the last resort in times of danger – hence its nickname 'Anchor of Salvation'.

The large number of anchors was needed not for normal anchoring but because they had to be expendable in emergencies. When speed of departure was the most vital factor then the cable was simply hacked through with axes and the ship sailed away leaving its anchor on the sea bed.

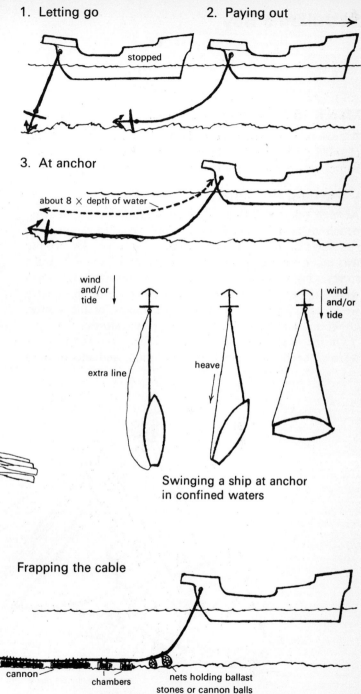

1. Letting go

2. Paying out

stopped

3. At anchor

about 8 × depth of water

wind and/or tide

extra line

heave

wind and/or tide

Swinging a ship at anchor in confined waters

Frapping the cable

cannon

chambers

nets holding ballast stones or cannon balls

St Julian's Bay

March 1520. 49 degrees South

A cross was set up on the highest hill and all the land was claimed in the name of Spain. Before the full force of the winter weather hit them it was decided to careen the ships.

Careening the ships

At high tide some ships were run aground on a shelving beach, as near broadside as possible. Wooden ramps were run down to the sand and the unloading began. Everything was taken ashore — all sails, the topmasts, spars, barrels, stores, cargo, personal belongings, armament — the ships were stripped of everything. Huts were made up from extra wood, and these became the crew's homes for the winter. Other huts and tarpaulin tents covered the stores and cargo.

On the next high tide one, or perhaps two, of the ships were rebeached even higher up the sand, and anchor lines

ashore heaved the now empty hulks broadside on to the beach. Long tackles were attached to the tops and set up ashore. As these were hauled tight the ships heeled over. Ropes and rope ladders were hung over the side, and soon the exposed curve of the hull was swarming with seamen. They scraped away at the months of sea growth — barnacles and sea 'grass'. Carpenters and caulkers examined the woodwork, much of it suffering from the attacks of sea worms. If no planks needed replacing then caulking could begin.

On the beach, fires were lit beneath iron pots and soon the crew were hurrying back and forth delivering boiling black pitch. After cleaning the loose stuff from the seams the caulkers hammered in rope fibers, and poured from ladles thin streams of pitch to make a perfect seal. This was the time of the caulkers, and the whole crew worked under their orders. All was speed. Hands or feet splashed with boiling tar

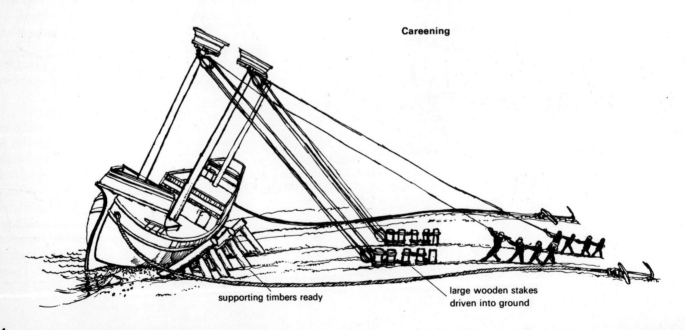

Careening

supporting timbers ready

large wooden stakes
driven into ground

had to be ignored. Columbus once careened and cleaned a ship between one high tide and the next, but in St. Julian there was more time — probably enough time to spend a few days on each ship.

Augers bored out the largest worm holes, and fresh treenails were hammered home. Areas that looked suspiciously weak were coated with pitch, and then lead sheeting was nailed over them. All was then coated with tallow and pitch. When the exposed side was completed the next high tide was awaited, the ship turned, and the whole process repeated for the other side of the hull.

Once careening was over, life settled down to a more leisurely pace. Foraging parties explored for a few miles inland. Huts were made more weather-proof with turf and old canvas. Permanent fires and cooking arrangements were made. Men made themselves comfortable for what could be a five-month stay.

When the weather permitted, the carpenters and caulkers continued their work on the upper parts of the ships while the crew cleaned out the holds. Rats were killed and their nests destroyed, the green scum from the bilges was hauled out in buckets, and the woodwork was washed down with water and vinegar. Attempts were made to clear the food store areas of cockroaches. Pure vinegar was used if the infestation was bad. Shore parties searched for bushes or herbs that might have fumigating properties. When dried, the branches and leaves were burned until the hold was full of smoke. It was hoped that the fumes would cut down the lice population of the ship.

Other sailors, under the boatswain and his mate, set to and aired the spare sails and patched the old ones. Others examined ropes for wear and either respliced worn parts or replaced them completely. Blocks were stripped down and greased with tallow. The whole of the upper section of the ships was well rubbed with fish oil, and painted sections were repainted. When the crew were painting or oiling they used rags held in the hand; for finer areas brushes made of a rope end did the job. Only the painter used the fine paint brushes.

Every day parties were detailed to fish and to hunt for food. Fresh water springs were found and marked on the Captain's and pilot's sketch maps. One day a search party discovered a new source of food — a camel without humps.

For the first time for many a month the contents of the sea-

The 'camel without humps' was either the llama, which the natives used as a beast of burden, or one of its relatives, the guanaco or the alpaca. This engraving represents a llama (left) and a guanaco.

men's chests were spread out, aired and deloused. Clothes were washed in fresh water and were no longer encrusted with salt grains. Without the smelling bilges and holds, without the fleas, cockroaches and rats, with fresh food and ample water, with space to walk and even run, the surgeon found that few men were sick. Everyone seemed to be a great deal healthier.

Gallows Point

All may have been healthy but some of the Captains and crew were unhappy with the whole trip and had lost the will to continue. They mutinied. A running fight ensued on the night of the first and second of April but the loyal crews held fast. Captain Luis de Mendoza, a mutineer, was stabbed to death and the others captured. The body of Mendoza was quartered and the parts set up on a beach – later to be known as Gallows Point. Captain Gaspar de Quesada was beheaded and quartered and Gallows Point gained more stakes. The ring leaders, Captain Juan de Cartagena and a priest, Father Pedro Sanchez de la Reina, were sentenced to be marooned at the first opportunity.

The Straits

The loss of the Santiago

Magellan ordered the *Santiago* to search southwards in hope of sighting the strait he was so sure existed. On 22 May the *Santiago* was caught by a sudden squall from the east and went full tilt on to a low sandbank. Away went sails and masts over the bows. Deck planking was shattered and the hull seams sprang wide open.

Luckily all the crew scrambled on to the sand bank. No-one was lost but they had to sit shivering while the seas turned their ship and belongings into pieces of driftwood. Two men managed to reach the shore and walk the 72 miles back to St Julian's Bay. It took them four days of trudging through rough thorny land with the temperature so low the only water they could get was by sucking pieces of ice. But make it they did, and the shipwrecked crew were saved.

The search continues

On 24 August 1520, when spring had come to the south, the fleet departed from St Julian and continued the search south-wards. Another large bay was discovered and named Santa Cruz and it was here on 8 October that they left the weeping and despairing Cartagena and the priest – nothing was ever heard of them again.

'On the 21st of October I took the altitude of the sun in exactly 52° South, at five leagues from the land, and there was an opening like a bay, and it has at the entrance, on the right hand a very long spit of sand, it is called the Cape of the Virgins . . . and within this bay we found a strait.' (From the log of Francisco Albo.)

The entrance did not look very promising but Pigafetta says that Magellan knew where to look and he sent the *San Antonio* and the *Concepcion* to explore. The *Trinidad* and the *Victoria* tried to anchor but the leadsman could find no bottom, so the ships tied up to the shore with their mooring ropes wrapped round prominent rocks.

For two days they waited anxiously. Then from round a bend came the *San Antonio* and the *Concepcion*. Their banners were flying, the crews cheering, and their cannons roaring. This was it – the strait.

The two ships had sailed on through a maze of dead-

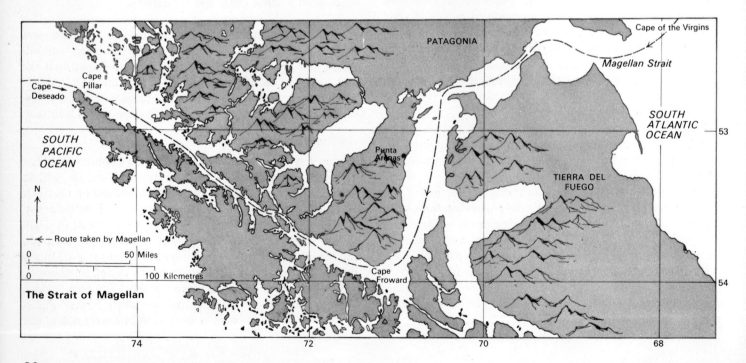

The Strait of Magellan

Cape of Virgins, seen from inside the Strait.

Cape Froward, at the junction of the east and west channels.

Cape Pillar and the exit to the Pacific seen from inside the Strait.

ends and twisting turns and still they found a tidal surge of water that tasted pure brine. There had been no need to go further.

It took another four weeks for the fleet to explore and finally reach the cape at the western entrance – they called it Cape Deseado (the Desired Cape). The land to the south was dotted with native fires at night and so was called Tierra del Fuego – the Land of Fire. The strait itself received many names:

The Channel of All Saints, the name given by Magellan.
The Strait of Victoria, named after the ship which first sighted it.
The Strait of the Mother of God.
The Strait of Martin Behaim, after a globe maker who hinted that it existed.
The Strait of Patagonia (Pathagonico) the name given by Pigafetta; the explorers had called the natives of the area *patagones* or big feet.

It was the rest of the world which decided to call it after Magellan.
There had been much searching back and forth in the twisting passages of the strait and when the fleet gathered together again they discovered that the *San Antonio* had disappeared.

After days of searching they gave up hope of finding her. Two banners were placed on prominent hills with messages buried in pots beneath them. It was hoped that the straying ship would find them and follow in the wake of the others. (The *San Antonio* had deserted, and was well on her way back to Spain when her absence was noted.)

28 November, 1520

The *Trinidad*, the *Concepcion*, and the *Victoria* entered the new ocean. The priests blessed the ships. Te Deums were sung, cannon were fired. Magellan addressed all who could hear: 'Gentlemen, we are now steering into waters where no ship has sailed before. May we always find them as peaceful as they are this morning. In this hope I shall name this sea the Mar Pacifico.'

The statue of Magellan in the modern town of Punta Arenas on the Strait.

Celestial navigation

Fixing position at sea

The navigators of the sixteenth century believed what they could see. They saw the earth as the centre of all things with a dome of stars as a timekeeper, direction finder, and a position finder.

Polaris

Stella Maris, the star of the sea. This was the most important star of all, the one we call the North Star, or Pole Star, or Polaris. It is a faint star and can only be seen north of the equator. But it is positioned practically above the earth's north pole. It rotates in a tiny circle above the pole and Pigafetta wrote about how to tell its error by using the pointers of the Plough (Big Dipper or Great Bear).

Other stars

A popular constellation, visible in northern and southern latitudes, was Orion's Belt. This quadrant of stars straddles the equator at all times and its central stars are due east and west when rising and setting.

The Southern Cross was a new sight to most of Magellan's men. It was good as a general direction guide but it swings in too large a circle to be of any use in accurate position finding.

Latitude by Polaris

Without understanding exactly why, they also knew that the altitude of Polaris above the horizon gave the latitude of the observer. They could tell how far North or South they were. If the Pole Star was on the horizon they were on the equator, if it was 37 degrees above, then they were in latitude 37 degrees, the latitude of Cape St Vincent; if 29 degrees, then latitude was 29 degrees, the latitude of the Canary Islands. The problem was how to measure this altitude while at sea.

On land, with large steady instruments and plumb lines, it was an easy task. But a ship's heaving deck rules out steady instruments of any type. Two instruments, however, were used on Magellan's voyage. One was the astrolabe. The other was the quadrant.

The astrolabe

The idea was to sight the star when the astrolabe was hung vertically – a nearly impossible task. It was best performed by two men. One suspended it by placing a thumb in the ring and holding it up. The other hand gently touched the ring, keeping it pointed in the right direction, and also adjusted the angle of the sight vane. The second man took the reading when ordered. A difficult task in gentle sea, it was a hopeless task in heavy seas. An error of one degree in reading meant an error of about sixty miles in latitude. Using the same astrolabe ashore the pilots expected to find their latitudes accurate to one third of a degree.

Using an astrolabe

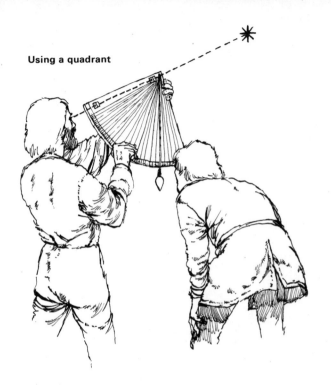

Using a quadrant

The quadrant

This was held firmly in the hand and the star sighted through the holes or along the upper edge. Any movements of the ship had to be counteracted by movements of the observer's body. A small plumb line indicated the reading and this usually had to be read by a second person. The momentum of the plumb line made this just as difficult to use as the astrolabe.

No other star could give such reliable information as did the Pole Star. Reluctantly the navigators in southern waters, no longer able to see Polaris, turned to the only other object in the sky which could help them find their position – the sun.

The sun for finding latitude

Locked away in the Captain-General's chest and used only by him and perhaps the pilot was a much prized possession. It was a book written by the astronomers at the Royal Observatory in Spain. Magellan may also have had similar books from the Portuguese observatories. The book gave the calculated height of the sun above the equator, at noon, for every day of the year, for four years in advance. If the altitude of the sun at noon could be found by observation, then by using these tables the latitude could be calculated.

If the altitude of Polaris caused trouble then that of the sun caused far more. It could only be taken at one time during the day, at noon, when at its highest point. It could not be sighted directly – the observer would be blinded. Sometimes a piece of smoked glass was held in line with the sight vane but this, too, was not an easy task. More usual was the method of holding a card behind the astrolabe. When the sight vane was in line with the sun then a tiny spot of light would appear on the card. It was a tricky manoeuvre, and since time keeping was not perfect, the observation had to start before noon and continue until the sun had risen to its highest point and started its downward path.

There can be no doubt that these navigators, when in southern seas, longed for the constant Stella Maris.

Using astrolabe and card

Longitude

We have considered how the navigators could, with luck, find their latitude – how far North or South they were. They had, however, no means of using instruments to find their longitude – how far East or West they were. They lacked knowledge of the true circumference of the world and, most important, they had no constant time-keeping device. Their hour glasses had to be reset at noon. These factors made accuracy impossible.

The only way left to find out where they were was to make a calculated guess. Starting from a known position they judged ocean currents, judged the drift to leeward of the ship, hoped that the course steered was accurate, found their latitude as often as possible, and tried to estimate the varying speeds of the ship and how far it had travelled. It was no wonder that the crew would often see the Master and pilot arguing not only about observed altitudes but also over the distance travelled and the exact position of the ship.

All the factors just mentioned, with the exception of latitude and compass course, had to be judged by experience. Seamen relied a great deal on the 'feel' of the ship under differing wind directions.

Speed judging was becoming a little more accurate. Still in use was the old method of throwing overboard at the bows something that would float, and watching it drift past. Sometimes they paced the deck, keeping abreast of the floating object, sometimes they timed its passage along the length of the ship with a small glass. But it is known that Magellan used a more accurate piece of apparatus. No details are known, but it was probably a forerunner of the chip log. The log with the pin pushed in by hand was thrown from the stern and the line paid out freely as it drifted astern. Once the log was clear of the turbulent water of the wake a knot would be nearing the hands of the seaman who was paying out the line. As he felt the knot pass through his fingers he shouted 'Now' and the sand glass was turned. The sailor then counted out aloud the number of knots that passed through his hands until the glass ran out. A good jerk on the line would then dislodge the wooden plug and so allow the apparatus to be hauled in easily.

A little mathematics will show that the distance between each knot can be related to the time of the sand glass which is related to one hour. So the number of knots counted will give the speed of the ship without having to do any further calcul-

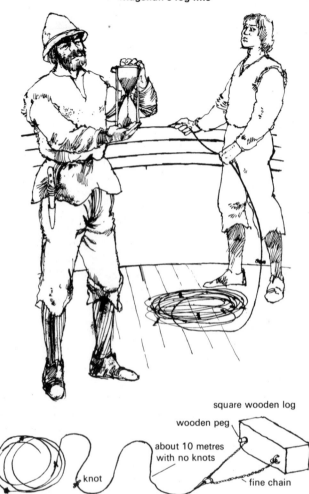

Magellan's log line

square wooden log

wooden peg

about 10 metres with no knots

knot

fine chain

Using modern measurements, a timer of one minute (1/60th of an hour) and knots spaced 1/60th of a nautical mile apart would give readings of nautical miles per hour.

ation. It must be remembered that this speed was the speed through water, not the speed over the solid seabed below. Tides and currents could be moving both the ship and the log in any number of directions.

During each hour of the day and night some record had to be kept of the courses steered and estimates of the distances run. It is possible that a slate was used but it is more likely that a simple visual method was employed – such as a traverse board which had rows of holes for the points of the compass with pegs to be inserted when the sand glass was turned. Again it is not known if Magellan sailed with one of these boards but it is possible. A traverse board is shown on p. 26.

Charts

World charts were, and still are, instruments for navigation. Magellan had his own charts, perhaps copied from those in the Portuguese observatories, and they were guarded like precious jewels. World charts were made up and drawn at the great navigation schools of either Spain or Portugal. Anyone found taking charts out of a country without permission was subject to the death penalty.

After Magellan's death his charts came into the custody of whoever was in charge of the fleet and in the end came to de Elcano who commanded the *Victoria* on her last leg home. Once back in Seville he handed them over to the King's officers. No one knows what became of those charts. We know nothing of their size or what information they contained. But by examining other charts of the period we can make a good guess.

Before Magellan set sail, the islands of the Caribbean had been explored and voyages as far south as the River Plate had been made, so he would certainly have had a chart.

This chart was made by Diego Ribero in 1529. He was a Portuguese employed by the King of Spain in 1526 to work on the official map kept in Seville. On that map, the *padron general*, all the latest discoveries in the New World were recorded. Ribero probably based this chart on the official map. By 1529 most of the east coast of America was known and details of the Pacific coast were beginning to come in.

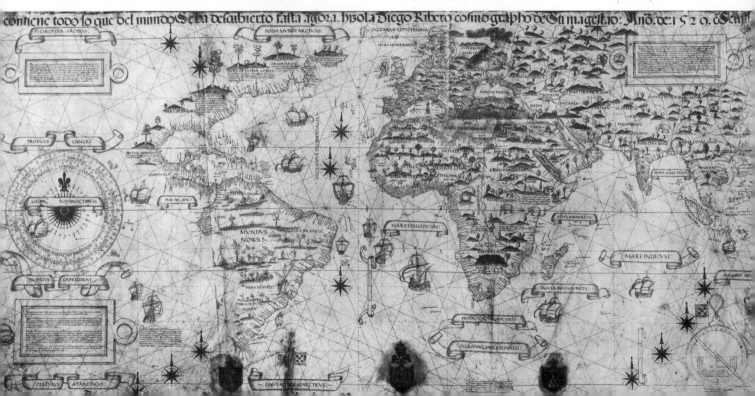

For all lands discovered Magellan would also have had books with sailing directions in them. The first picture shows part of a page from an English book of sailing directions called a 'rutter.' It describes the island of Ushant, off France.

Item, when you are northwest and by north of Ushant then maye you see through the poynte which is to the southwarts of the maine Iland, and when you are of of Ushant northwest and by west, then is that poynt shutte in on the shore.

Vshiant

Item, when Ushant beares north northwest from you, then doth it appeere like as it is heere aboue demonstrated.
Item, when you are off of Ushant Northwest and by west, or west northwest then lyes there a great Rocke of

When new coastlines were found important bays and headlands were added in the blank spaces on charts, if their latitude was known. All the finer details, descriptions, drawings, soundings were noted down in books. Often these books contained simple drawings of special areas. The next picture is a sketch made by Pigafetta, who was not a navigator, of the strait discovered by Magellan.

The world charts were not used to plot the ship's position hour by hour, or even watch by watch. A good day's run would often be less than a centimetre on such a scale of chart. Once the ship's position had been calculated, usually at noon, it was pricked on the chart with the point of a pair of compasses. This pinprick would give a rough idea where they were in relation to the land. A ruler laid from the pinprick would also show the next course to steer.

Finding the course to steer

There were no lines of latitude and longitude on the charts, but compass roses were placed at strategic positions and the points, 32 of them, were extended to cover the chart. These extended lines were often of differing colours and the points of the ship's compass were painted to match these colours.

From the pinprick of the ship's position the ruler was laid to the destination. If the edge of the ruler coincided with a ray from a compass then this was the course to steer. It was identified by tracing it back to its rose or by its colour. If it did not coincide then a pair of compasses was opened out and one point

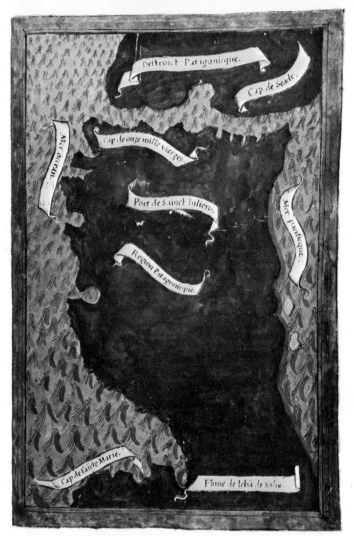

Pigafetta's sketch of the Strait. South is at the top.

slid along the ruler. The other point sought out a ray that was parallel. When an exact parallel could not be found the navigator had to take the next best as the drawing opposite shows. This then would be the course to steer. This simple method served a captain very well, so long as the charts were reasonably accurate. It had helped Magellan to cross the Atlantic, for example. But once through the straits and into the Pacific it brought near disaster because the charts were wrong.

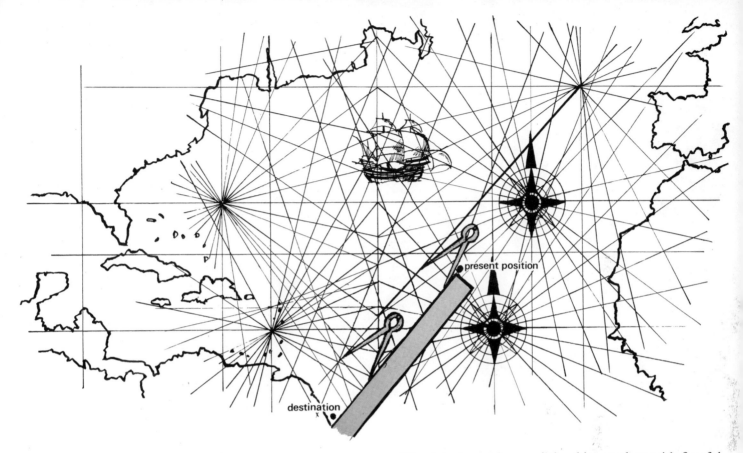

present position

destination

The Pacific diet: no land, no food, no drink

On Wednesday 28 November the *Concepcion*, the *Trinidad* and the *Victoria* sailed out into the newly named Pacific Ocean.

Magellan thought the worst was over. He had found the elusive strait and all that remained was a few weeks' easy sailing to the islands of the East.

It was to be three months and twenty days before fresh food and water were found.

As the weeks rolled by and no land appeared the remaining food was strictly rationed and fishing lines streamed continuously from all points of the ships. Spare sails were draped over the deck equipment to form hollows to collect rain or dew.

The days dragged on and the ships sped on with fine following winds. The biscuits turned into heaps of maggot-ridden dust but were eaten thankfully. The water turned yellow and putrid and the daily ration could be swallowed in one gulp. Men prayed as they had never prayed before, but still no land appeared.

The crew were growing weaker each day, so while some strength remained, the ship's boats were lowered and towed astern. They would be needed when land was found and a few weak men could manage to anchor the ships but not get the large launch over the side. Then some of the crew's gums began to swell and bleed. Teeth became loose and fell out, tongues blackened – and men died. The bodies were wrapped in their sleeping sheets or bags and, while the ships moved on, were dropped overboard. Without weights the bundles sank slowly and sharks began to follow in the wake of the ships.

Pigafetta's sketch of the island of thieves. His drawing of a ship seems to be trying to show the double canoes, or outriggers, used by the natives.

One day islands were sighted and salvation seemed near. But as they drew close no bottom could be found with the lead and the islands looked treeless and barren. The task of sailing past, turning about, and tacking in close was beyond their strength. They had no choice but to keep on going.

The ships were searched for scraps of food, and even the carpenter's sawdust was eaten. Anyone catching a rat could sell it for a gold piece.

Finally the leather coverings from the yards, which prevented them chafing against the shrouds, were stripped off. Being weatherhardened, it needed preparation before eating. The leather was cut into strips and towed through the sea for a few days. This treatment softened it up and it was then lightly grilled. All leather fittings were cooked in this way and shared amongst the crew.

Still no land appeared – the men grew weaker still – more and more men died.

Wednesday 6 March 1521. Land sighted. The crews cheered, sank to their knees and chanted the *Laudate Domine*.

However even these islands, now called the Marianas, proved a disappointment. After a running fight with the thieving natives the ships left on 9 March. They finally found haven in a group of islands now known as the Philippines. Tents were set up on a small island near Saman Island on 16 March.

The Philippines

The 150 survivors had sailed halfway round the world and it was rumoured that Magellan had actually circumnavigated the globe since he was said to have visited the Philippines many years before.

With ample supplies of pigs, eggs, fruit, fish and fresh water the weary crews began to recover their strength. Soon the fleet moved on among the islands. Magellan met many important chiefs and tried to persuade them to become allies of the King of Spain. He was successful. Hundreds of natives became converts to Christianity, though it is not likely that they really understood much about this new religion.

44

The Battle of Mactan. Saturday 27 April 1521

The previous night Magellan had asked for volunteers to make an attack on a nearby heathen island. The volunteers were to put on a display to show how Christian men could overwhelm the superior forces of those who refused Christ's teachings. Friendly local chieftains who were now Christians were to accompany the small army but would take no part in the fighting. They would watch at a distance, for this was a show of strength by Europeans.

Armed with crossbows, swords and lances – and the occasional hand gun – the sixty 'soldiers' were rowed to the island and dawn found them off shore from a sloping sandy beach. Rocks prevented the launches from approaching any nearer so the men were ordered into the water. It only reached their waists but it was a long wade to the distant shore and trees.

As they neared the shore hundreds of Philippine warriors appeared from the trees. They were waving swords, scimitars and wooden lances, and by the time the little army stood on dry sand their enemies numbered more than a thousand. Pigafetta, who was with the party, recorded that there were more than 1500 of them.

The yelling warriors charged. The guns and crossbows in the seamen's inexperienced hands were of little use. The islanders pressed their attack more vigorously. Now they aimed at the seamen's unprotected legs. Leaping and dodging, with shields held forward, the natives closed in. Spears thrust at eyes and swords slashed at legs. Before the onrush the small group backed knee deep into the sea.

Then Magellan was down, a leg and arm badly slashed. Joyful enemies screamed their triumph and crowded round his body slashing and stabbing.

Frightened and bewildered, soaked and bloodstained, the volunteers splashed hurriedly back to the safety of the boats. Eight of their number were dead and nearly all bore some wound or other. But most shattering of all – Magellan was dead. The enemy were still hacking at the corpse.

Sadly the survivors rowed away. The sun had barely cleared the horizon.

Although this portrait is supposed to be Magellan it was made many years after his death and nobody really knows what he looked like. We do know that this was his signature. It appears on a letter he wrote to the King of Spain in October 1518.

Pigafetta's sketch of the Spice Islands.

The last lap

After the death of Magellan there were months of undecided and troublesome wanderings amongst the islands before the two surviving ships and 115 men finally found the Spice Islands. The *Concepcion* had leaked so badly that all valuable stuff had been transferred to the *Victoria* and *Trinidad*, and then she had been burned.

Much bartering took place; even seamen swapped shirts for packets of cloves. Then the two ships were ready to sail, fully loaded with the most valuable cargo of all, cloves and cinnamon. Suddenly the *Trinidad* was found to be leaking. As her seamen pumped they saw clear and pure sea water pouring from the pumps. She was in no fit condition to attempt the long run around the Cape of Good Hope. Since the winds were favourable it was decided that the *Victoria* with 47 men and 13 natives, under the command of Elcano, would attempt the voyage alone. They set sail on 2 December 1521. Later the *Trinidad* was repaired and tried the Pacific crossing to Panama. She failed, was driven back, and was captured by a Portuguese fleet.

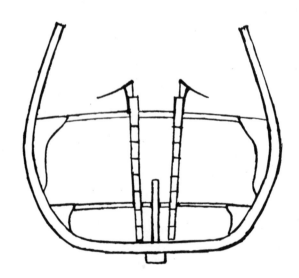

A bulkhead running the length of the hold and about a metre high prevented water running from side to side and so making the ship unstable. Because of this bulkhead two pumps were required, one on each side.

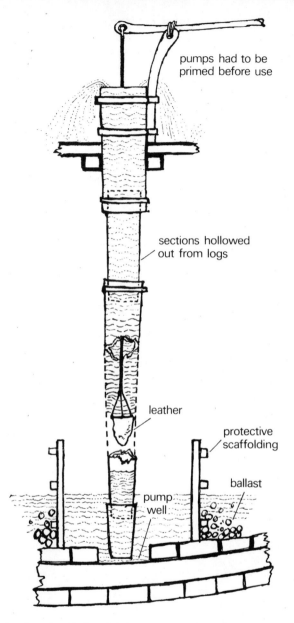

pumps had to be primed before use

sections hollowed out from logs

leather

protective scaffolding

ballast

pump well

As the leather rises it fits tightly, pushes up a column of water which spills out at the top, and creates a vacuum which sucks up more water.

Condensation and seepage through the seams was only slight in a 'tight' ship — enough to fill the pumps' well once a day. A few strokes on the pumps each morning would soon draw up the dirty water on to the deck where it would run to the scuppers. Once a ship had developed leaks the pumps would bring up large quantities of clear sea water. Such a ship would be unfit for a long ocean passage.

Elcano's decision to return home via the Cape was a desperate venture. His ship was worn and weather beaten, its timbers eaten by marine growths and patched with sheeting, treenails and tar. The running rigging was beginning to rot and made up of odd sections joined by splicing, the sails were patched and threadbare. The only ports on the African coast were in the hands of the Portuguese, and their fleets made regular passages around the Cape of Good Hope. His only chance was to sail well south, into the face of the strong Westerlies and then head North into mid Atlantic. It would be a voyage of nearly 13,000 miles without calling in at any port.

The *Victoria* headed well south of the Cape to avoid contact with the Portuguese shipping and it was not until 6 May 1522 that she managed to double the Cape against strong westerly winds.

As they sailed into the Atlantic the last of the meat was gone, most of it putrified through lack of salt. Their diet was now only rice.

Twenty men died of starvation and it became obvious that without food they would never reach Spain. So on 9 July the *Victoria* put into the Cape Verde Islands. They spread the story that they had come from America and kept their cargo a secret, for these were Portuguese islands. Supplies were taken on board, but someone let the truth out and the ship had to leave hurriedly – with thirteen of her crew still ashore.

On Monday 8 September 1522 the *Victoria* dropped anchor in the harbour at Seville. On Tuesday eighteen barefoot men, the only survivors, walked through the streets to give thanks at the shrine of Santa Maria. It had been three years and 40,000 miles ago that 234 men had sailed out in five gaily decorated ships.

The cargo of spices paid for all the ships and wages and still left a fantastic profit. For the backers it had been a very successful voyage indeed.

We do not have a list of the names of the 234 men who sailed in 1519 but we do have a list of the 18 who made it back to Seville in 1522.

Juan Sebastian de Elcano	Master
Francisco Albo (Alvo)	Pilot
Miguel de Rodas	Pilot
Juan de Acurio	Pilot
Antonio Pigafetta	Unpaid supernumerary
Martin de Judicibus	Chief steward
Hernando de Bustamente	Mariner (barber)
Nicolas the Greek	Mariner
Miguel Sanchez	Mariner
Antonio Hernandez Colmenero	Mariner
Francisco Rodrigues	Mariner
Juan Rodrigues	Mariner
Diego Carmena	Mariner
Hans of Aachen	Gunner
Juan de Arratia	Leading seaman
Vasco Gomez Galego	Leading seaman
Juan de Santandres	Apprentice seaman
Juan de Zubilita	Page. (He was 14 years old when he joined the fleet.)

◄ This globe is the earliest known map showing the route of Magellan's voyage. It was made about 1526, probably in Nuremberg. Twelve sections, printed on paper, were mounted on a solid wooden ball, There is now a crack in the ball.

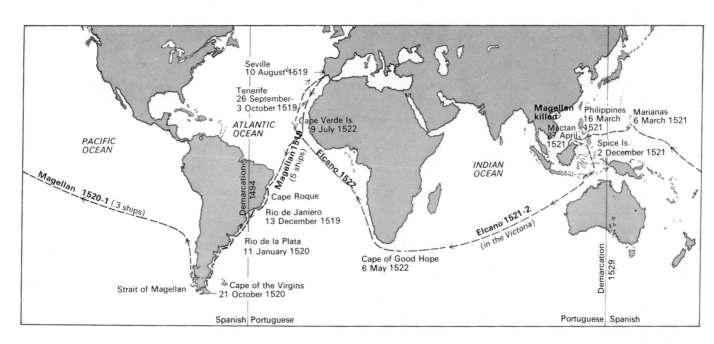

PACIFIC
OCEAN

ATLANTIC
OCEAN

INDIAN
OCEAN

Seville
10 August 1519

Tenerife
26 September-
3 October 1519

Cape Verde Is.
9 July 1522

Magellan killed
Mactan
27 April
1521

Philippines
16 March
1521

Marianas
6 March 1521

Spice Is.
2 December 1521

Magellan 1519
(5 ships)

Elcano 1522

Magellan 1520-1 (3 ships)

Demarcation 1494

Cape Roque

Rio de Janiero
13 December 1519

Rio de la Plata
11 January 1520

Strait of Magellan

Cape of the Virgins
21 October 1520

Cape of Good Hope
6 May 1522

Elcano 1521-2
(in the Victoria)

Demarcation 1529

Spanish | Portuguese

Portuguese | Spanish

This modern map shows the route that Magellan
followed on his historic journey. The voyage lasted
three long years, and at its end, only 18 men were
left alive to describe the hardships the travellers had
endured and the wonders they had seen.

Index

Acknowledgments

Illustrations in this book are reproduced by kind permission of the following: p. 5 (right) from B. Landström, *The Ship*, Interbook Publishing AB; pp. 16, 37 (top), 42 (top left), 45 photographs by Cambridge University Library; p. 21 Ampliaciones y Reproducciones Mas; pp. 25, J. Allan Cash; p. 27 map based on Admiralty Chart by permission of the Controller HMSO and the Hydrographer of the Navy; pp. 31 (seal), 35 Natural History Museum; p. 31 Zoological Society of London; p. 37 (bottom right) Peter Wadhams, Scott Polar Research Institute, Cambridge; pp. 42, 44, 46, 48 Beinecke Rare Book and Manuscript Library, Yale University; p. 41 Biblioteca Apostolica Vaticana.

Drawings and cover illustrations by Graham Humphreys.

The front cover shows the start of the greatest of all the voyages of discovery. The artist has reconstructed the scene as Magellan's fleet bravely sailed from Seville to seek a way past America to the East Indies, the rich Spice Islands.

The back cover shows the home-coming. Only one worn ship made the whole voyage, but that ship had completely encircled the world.

The Cambridge History Library

The Cambridge Introduction to History
Written by Trevor Cairns

PEOPLE BECOME CIVILIZED

THE ROMANS AND THEIR EMPIRE

BARBARIANS, CHRISTIANS, AND MUSLIMS

THE MIDDLE AGES

EUROPE AND THE WORLD

THE BIRTH OF MODERN EUROPE

THE OLD REGIME AND THE REVOLUTION

POWER FOR THE PEOPLE

The Cambridge Topic Books
General Editor Trevor Cairns

THE AMERICAN WAR OF INDEPENDENCE
by R. E. Evans

BENIN: AN AFRICAN KINGDOM AND CULTURE
by Kit Elliott

THE BUDDHA
by F. W. Rawding

BUILDING THE MEDIEVAL CATHEDRALS
by Percy Watson

THE EARLIEST FARMERS AND THE FIRST CITIES
by Charles Higham

THE FIRST SHIPS AROUND THE WORLD
by W. D. Brownlee

HERNAN CORTES: CONQUISTADOR IN MEXICO
by John Wilkes

LIFE IN A FIFTEENTH-CENTURY MONASTERY
by Anne Boyd

LIFE IN THE IRON AGE
by Peter J. Reynolds

LIFE IN THE OLD STONE AGE
by Charles Higham

MARTIN LUTHER
by Judith O'Neill

THE MURDER OF ARCHBISHOP THOMAS
by Tom Corfe

MUSLIM SPAIN
by Duncan Townson

THE PYRAMIDS
by John Weeks

THE ROMAN ARMY
by John Wilkes

ST. PATRICK AND IRISH CHRISTIANITY
by Tom Corfe

The Cambridge History Library will be expanded in the future to include additional volumes. Lerner Publications Company is pleased to participate in making this excellent series of books available to a wide audience of readers.

Lerner Publications Company
241 First Avenue North, Minneapolis, Minnesota 55401